CONSIDER THE SOURCE

FINDING RELIABLE INFORMATION ON THE INTERNET

Paige Taylor and Jerri Lejeune

Fort Atkinson, Wisconsin

Many thanks to Isaac Golino, Paul Schenker and Mark Versaggi for their technical consultation, and Beth Walker, Nvart Stepanian and Aleshchai Herndon of the City of Pasadena (CA) Library System for their consultation and contributions.

Published by UpstartBooks
W5527 Highway 106
P.O. Box 800
Fort Atkinson, Wisconsin 53538-0800
1-800-448-4887

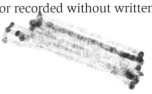

Table of Contents

Introduction for Teachers

A student comes up to you and excitedly tells you that Elvis Presley is still alive. In fact, she adds, someone saw him just last week in Colorado. She sees you wince and says, "No, really it's true. I read it on the Internet and there were even pictures of him."

As educators, we're used to explaining to students about unreliable sources of information, such as some of the tabloids infamous for their exaggerations and blatantly false claims. That's been a manageable task; we've been able to point out sources by name and caution students to be wary of what they read at supermarket checkouts.

We've also been able to lead them to textbooks and library resources they can trust. Not only do educators and librarians screen these sources, but also we take comfort in trusting publishers, knowing that they back their material with their reputations. However, now we're faced with a special challenge—the Internet.

The Internet is at once a dream and a nightmare for a student learning to do research. Part of its beauty is that it is so open; anyone can post anything they want on Web sites, and chat rooms are terrific forums for exchanging information and ideas. But while the Internet has become an indispensable tool for research and communication, it is largely unmonitored and thus ripe for inaccurate material—hoaxes, scams, farces and misinformation that is well intended. There are safeguards that can be used to keep children from accessing illicit sites on the Internet, but there are no mechanisms to keep them from reading (and believing) misinformation. Sometimes it's even hard for adults to tell what is valid and what is not.

The purpose of this book is to present fourth through sixth graders with strategies for learning how and where to find reliable sources on the Internet, how to recognize questionable information and how to verify it. Not only will these abilities strengthen their research skills, they will learn critical thinking skills. They will be more skeptical about unverified facts and more aware of biases in their sources. Considering that they will encounter many things on the Internet that we will never know about, such skills become especially important.

How to Use This Book

Chapter 1 begins with an overview of the Internet. Students will build a basic vocabulary and develop a general understanding of how the Internet works. They will also realize the impossibility of monitoring the Internet for accuracy and the importance of checking out their sources. Chapters 2–7 contain the evaluation criteria students need when analyzing Web sites. Chapter 8 discusses the two other areas of the Internet students in the fourth through sixth grades most commonly access—chat rooms and e-mail. Chapters 9 and 10 suggest research applications that will help students use what they have learned.

Each chapter includes:

- games, activities and/or exercises (class, small group and/or individual)
- correlations with the National Educational Technology Standards (NETS) for Students (These standards were developed by the International Society for Technology in Education, and they have been adopted, or acknowledged, in state board of education documents by

82% of the state boards of education.) Further information on the National Standards can be found at their Web site, www.iste.org. Every national standard is met at least twice. For ease in evaluating the scope of this book, a complete scope and sequence chart is provided in Appendix A on pages 109–110.

As students evaluate Web sites, they can use either of the checklists on pages 8–9 to determine the usefulness of the site. The example below specifies where each item on the checklist can be found in this book.

Domain Names		
• Did the domain name help you quickly determine the basic content of the site?	Lesson 2	Y N NA
• Is the purpose of the site clear? Is it an organization, government, military, education or commercial Web site?	Lesson 2	Y N NA
Authority		
• Is the author of the Web site clearly identified?	Lesson 1	Y N NA
• Is information about the author available?	Lesson 1	Y N NA
• Does the author have the appropriate credentials and/or expertise?	Lesson 2	Y N NA
• Is the sponsor of the Web site clearly identified?	Lesson 3	Y N NA
• Is contact information for the author or sponsor available?	Lesson 3	Y N NA
Currency		
• Is the latest revision date provided? If so, what is it? _____	Lesson 1	Y N NA
• Is the latest revision date appropriate to the material?	Lesson 1	Y N NA
• Is the Web site content updated frequently?	Lesson 1	Y N NA
• Are links to other Web sites current?	Lesson 1	Y N NA
• Is the grammar and spelling correct?	Sidebar	Y N NA
Verifiability		
• Is the information accurate based on your knowledge of the subject?	Lesson 1	Y N NA
• Is the information consistent with similar information in other sources?	Lesson 1	Y N NA
Bias		
• Is the content of the site clear?	Lesson 1	Y N NA
• Is the content well organized?	Lesson 1	Y N NA
• Is the information easy to understand?	Lesson 1	Y N NA
• Is the content free of bias? If not, can the bias be easily detected?	Lesson 2, 3, 4	Y N NA
Misinformation		
• Is the Web site a hoax?	Lesson 1, 2	Y N NA
• Is the Web site a spoof?	Lesson 3	Y N NA
• Does the Web site discuss paranormal phenomena?	Lesson 4	Y N NA

Introduction for Students

When you see something in writing, do you always trust it? If you read it in a library book or in a textbook, your answer is probably "yes." After all, library materials and texts have been carefully selected and screened by people whose job it is to be concerned with accuracy.

What if you are in the supermarket at the checkout and you see a magazine headline that reads "Mother gives birth to alien triplets"? You probably laugh when you realize it's on the front of one of those tabloids known for ridiculous claims. So, of course, just because something is in print, doesn't mean it is necessarily true.

What about the Internet? Can you trust everything you read there? Think of all the information you can get from Web sites, chat rooms and sometimes even e-mail. Can you believe it all? The answer is, *not everything*. The Internet contains all kinds of information entered by all kinds of people. Much of it is true, but some of it is only partly true, and some of it is utterly false. This book will help you learn to think carefully about what you read and show you how to check out questionable information.

Consider the Source
Evaulation Criteria for Web Sites

Site Title: _____

Subject: _____

URL:_____

Domain Names			
• Did the domain name help you quickly determine the basic content of the site?	Y	N	NA
• Is the purpose of the site clear? Is it an organization, government, military, education or commercial Web site?	Y	N	NA
Authority			
• Is the author of the Web site clearly identified?	Y	N	NA
• Is information about the author available?	Y	N	NA
• Does the author have the appropriate credentials and/or expertise?	Y	N	NA
• Is the sponsor of the Web site clearly identified?	Y	N	NA
• Is contact information for the author or sponsor available?	Y	N	NA
Currency			
• Is the latest revision date provided? If so, what is it? _____	Y	N	NA
• Is the latest revision date appropriate to the material?	Y	N	NA
• Is the Web site content updated frequently?	Y	N	NA
• Are links to other Web sites current?	Y	N	NA
• Is the grammar and spelling correct?	Y	N	NA
Verifiability			
• Is the information accurate based on your knowledge of the subject?	Y	N	NA
• Is the information consistent with similar information in other sources?	Y	N	NA
Bias			
• Is the content of the site clear?	Y	N	NA
• Is the content well organized?	Y	N	NA
• Is the information easy to understand?	Y	N	NA
• Is the content free of bias? If not, can the bias be easily detected?	Y	N	NA
Misinformation			
• Is the Web site a hoax?	Y	N	NA
• Is the Web site a spoof?	Y	N	NA
• Does the Web site discuss paranormal phenomena?	Y	N	NA

Consider the Source

✔ Check It Out! ✔

Answer the questions for each of the categories for your Web site. Put a check in the box on the left when you are done.

	Authority of Source	• Who is the author? _____ • Does he/she give credentials or tell why his/her experience qualifies him/her to write the article?* ❑ Yes ❑ No
	Up to Date?	• Does this information need to be current? ❑ Yes ❑ No • If so, when was the page last updated? Date: _____
	Purpose	• Is the purpose to give information? ❑ Yes ❑ No • Is the purpose to sell something?** ❑ Yes ❑ No • Is the purpose to entertain? ❑ Yes ❑ No • Is the purpose to promote an idea?** ❑ Yes ❑ No
	Other Sources	• Have you found other sites that confirm the information? ❑ Yes ❑ No • Are there books or magazines that agree with this site's facts? ❑ Yes ❑ No
	Spelling and Grammar	• Did the author use correct spelling and grammar in their writing?* ❑ Yes ❑ No
	Other	• What was your general impression of the web site? (circle one) **Poor Fair Good Very Good Excellent**

* If you answered "no," confirm your information with another source.

** If you answered "yes," confirm your information with another source.

The Internet: Who's at the Controls?

This chapter provides basic information on the Internet that will serve as your students' foundation for the balance of the book. The chapter contains three lessons. The first is a warm-up review—you will discover how much your students already know about the Internet, while they will refine their definitions of Internet terms. The second lesson gives a brief history of the Internet and explains that there is no way to monitor its accuracy. The third lesson discusses the issue of Internet monitoring.

Terms Introduced

- censorship
- chat room
- editor
- e-mail
- Internet
- Internet Service Provider (ISP)
- Local Area Network (LAN)
- misinformation
- publication
- questionable

Lesson Plan 1

Components of the Internet

NET Standards Covered: 1a and 2c

Objectives: Students will be able to:

- define the Internet
- identify the most commonly used systems on the Internet
- evaluate hypothetical situations and identify Internet system to be used

■ Autograph Activity

Materials:

- chalkboard

- Autograph Activity worksheet for each student (see page 17)
- overhead of Autograph Activity to record student responses
- chart paper for recording answers and discoveries
- timer

Time: Approximately 30 minutes

Directions:

1. Provide students with a copy of the Autograph Activity.

2. Each box contains a phrase and room for an "autograph." Have students take 5–10 minutes to walk and talk, getting signatures from each other in as many boxes as possible. For example, if a student wrote an e-mail last night, he or she can sign the upper left hand box on another student's grid. The "winner" is the student with the most signatures when the timer goes off. No student may sign more than one box on the same grid. This keeps students moving and ensures that they won't get caught in conversation.

3. Set the timer and let the students begin.

4. When the timer goes off, students should immediately return to their seats. Have students count how many boxes are filled on their worksheets. Determine the winners by a show of hands.

■ Discussion

Ask your students if they have used e-mail, surfed the Web or "talked" in a chat room. Record the answers on an overhead transparency, the chalkboard or a piece of chart paper. These answers will reveal how Internet "savvy" your students are.

Ask what all of these activities have in common. The students should realize that all of the activities are part of the Internet. Ask students what the Internet is and write their answers on the board.

Next ask how people all over the world, sitting at their individual computers, actually communicate with each other. Accept all reasonable answers. Be sure that the students understand the following key points:

- Computers talk to each other using electronic signals.

- In order to "talk" to another computer, the electrical signals must pass back and forth from one computer to the next.

- This can happen when computers belong to a Local Area Network (LAN), such as the computers in a school, or through direct connections with the Internet.

- In order to communicate with computers that are not part of your own Local Network, signals must pass through "routers"—devices that can direct messages to their final destinations.

- For the most part the above happens automatically without monitoring by humans.

If you like, use the following metaphor to help clarify for your students the way computers connect to each other.

Imagine for a moment that all the students at our school had computers on their desks. Now imagine that the computers in each classroom were connected so that students could send information back and forth to each other within their classroom. That would be a Local Area Network (LAN).

Now picture cables connecting the classrooms together so that all of the classroom networks were linked. Any student in any classroom could send information to any other student at the school. That system would be a network of networks. On a gigantic scale, that's basically how the Internet works, connecting thousands and thousands of smaller networks throughout

the world. Just like the telephone system joins small networks to bigger ones and allows voice communication throughout the world, the Internet permits us to share written information with each other worldwide. We can even communicate over the Internet with our voices by using microphones and special software.

When information is sent through the Internet, special computers called routers direct the information to its destination. There are no people who control the information sent over the Internet. It is all done automatically with electronics.

■ Spider Web Activity

Have students build a physical model of Internet communication for a Local Area Network.

Materials:

- a ball of different colored yarn for each row or group

Time: Approximately 10 minutes

Directions:

1. Designate each row of students as its own network. Ask for four or five students to volunteer to act as routers. It is easiest if they stand at different points within the rows and are not too close to the other routers.

2. Give a different colored ball of yarn to the first student in each row. These students hold the end of the yarn and throw the ball to anyone in their own row. The receivers hold a piece of the yarn and toss the ball to another person in the row, etc.

3. To connect the rows (local area networks), students should throw the ball of yarn to the closest available router, who then throws it to a player in another row.

4. Play until all rows have been interconnected. **Note:** Yarn will likely be too tangled to wind up again.

Follow-up:

Check for understanding by asking students questions such as:

- "Could Jane (in row 1) send a message directly to Fred (in row 5)? Why not?" *No, the message must go through the router because they are not in the same Local Area Network.*

- "Who can Sam send a direct message to?" *Others in his Local Area Network.*

Continue questioning until you are sure that all of the students understand.

■ Internet Background

The most common types of communication on the Internet are:

- **e-mail**—allows users to send messages back and forth to each other at their convenience

- **chat rooms**—where users can have real time discussions with each other

- **World Wide Web**—a huge electronic library full of information files

What's the difference between the Internet and the World Wide Web?

Often people use the two terms to mean the same thing. However, technically the Internet refers to the message network, which allows transmission of WWW files as well as messages from chat rooms, e-mail and other systems. The Web is the biggest part of the system the Internet supports, e-mail and chat rooms being two other portions of the Internet. For a discussion of these and other Internet terms, visit www.webopedia.com.

Discussion Questions:

- If you are on the World Wide Web are you on the Internet too? *Yes*

- If you are on the Internet are you necessarily on the Web? *No*

■ Tangled Communications Activity

Materials:

- overhead of Tangled Communications (see page 18)

Directions:

1. Place the Tangled Communications transparency on the overhead.

2. Challenge each row or group to see how fast they can match the communication format

with its proper definition. After a minute ask a volunteer from each group to report on their decisions.

3. Compare students' choices to the real answers.

■ Additional Activity

Refer to the notes from the Autograph Activity and let students discuss the chat rooms they visit, their e-mail host and their favorite Web sites. Alternately, give each group a piece of chart paper divided in fourths and let them record the information from their group. Invite each group to the front to share their results.

■ Homework

Evaluate students' comprehension by having them complete the Internet Systems worksheet on page 19 or the A-maze-ing Message Machine worksheet on page 20 in class or as homework. Answers are on page 111.

Lesson Plan 2

History and Current Issues

NET Standards Covered: 1a, 2b, 2c. 3 and 5

This lesson provides a brief history of the Internet, emphasizing its newness, importance and potential for both positive and negative impacts. Students will become familiar with key points in Internet history and will complete a small group research project to learn the history of innovations in communication.

Objectives: Students will be able to:

- order historical events related to the Internet

- use the Internet to research the history of communication in small groups

■ Internet Facts Activity

Materials:

- Internet Fact Sheet (see page 21)

- 1 sheet each of several colors of paper (There will be one group of seven students per sheet of paper, so divide your class size by seven to determine how many different colored sheets you will need.)

Time: 10 minutes

Directions:

1. Copy the Internet Fact Sheet onto different colors of paper.

2. Cut the sheets apart so that there is one fact on each slip of paper.

3. Divide the class into groups of seven students. (Have extra students double up.)

4. Pass out the slips in random order, one per student.

5. Explain to the students that when you say "go," they should walk around the room and read their historical fact to as many other students as possible. When the whistle blows, they should stop talking and form groups according to their colors.

6. The students should line up so their facts are in chronological order.

7. The first students in each line should read their facts aloud and compare to see if the groups made the same decisions about what fact comes first. Continue until all seven facts are in order.

Optional: You might also have the whole paragraph on an overhead, and only uncover the sentences after each group reads them out loud. This will help students confirm their answers.

Alternate Activity:

Cut and paste the facts from the Internet Fact Sheet in random order on a sheet of paper and hand it out to students. Have the students number the facts in the correct order.

■ Group Research Project

Materials:

- computers
- research materials

Time: Approximately 3 class periods

Directions:

1. Divide the class into groups of five students each, assigning each group one of the following invention topics:

- telegraph
- telephone
- radio
- television
- space satellite
- fax machine

If there are more than 30 students in your class, add more inventions. If fewer, leave out one or more inventions.

2. Ask each group to research the following questions for their invention:

- who the inventor(s) was/were
- when the technology was invented
- what communication was like before the invention
- how communication was improved by the invention
- if and how the invention paved the way for the development of computers and/or the Internet

3. Each group should prepare a poster about their invention, and make a presentation to the class that includes the answers to their research questions.

4. After all of the groups have given their presentations, discuss which invention students think has been the most important for communication. Discuss how the Internet has improved communication throughout the world.

■ Class Discussion or Homework

Are there any drawbacks to the speed with which we can now communicate around the world? *Examples that could be cited: rushing information without thoughtful planning, sending out misinformation that spreads before it can be stopped, etc.*

The Issue of Internet Monitoring

NET Standard Covered: 2a

Objective: Students will learn that Internet monitoring is impossible with current technology.

■ Who's Watching Activity

Materials:

• Who's Watching? worksheet (see page 22)

Time: Approximately 15 minutes

Directions:

1. Review the following vocabulary words with your students:

   • **editor**—someone who reads over and corrects material in preparation for publication

   • **misinformation**—false or misleading information

   • **transmit**—to send something over an electronic system

   • **censorship**—the act of restricting material from publication or distribution

2. Pass out the activity sheet and ask the students to fill in the missing words so that the document makes sense. If desired, assign the activity as homework before the lesson.

3. Correct and discuss the activity sheet. Poll students to determine whether or not they think closer monitoring of the Internet is a good idea. The following extension activity offers the opportunity to develop critical thinking and oral language skills.

Extension Activity:

Pretend that there was some sort of new technology that could detect false or misleading information sent over the Internet. Debate a proposed new law that will permit the government to use this technology to censor information on the Internet.

■ Check Your Memory Activity

Materials:

• Check Your Memory crossword puzzle (see page 23)

Time: Approximately 15 minutes

Directions:

1. Pass out the crossword puzzle. Have the students complete it as a chapter review in class or as homework.

2. Check the answers as a class.

Note: If you are using the puzzle with younger students, you may want to provide the following words in a word bank.

CENSORSHIP	MISINFORMATION
CHAT ROOM	MONITOR
EDIT	NETWORK
E-MAIL	PUBLICATION
INTERNET	ROUTER
ISP	TRANSMIT
LAN	WEB

Key Concepts in Chapter 1

- The Internet is a huge information and message network that connects smaller networks around the world.

- E-mail, chat rooms and the World Wide Web are the most commonly used systems on the Internet.

- There is no way to monitor information on the Internet for accuracy. It is the responsibility of the Internet user to verify questionable material.

Autograph Activity

Wrote an e-mail last night _____	Received an e-mail last night _____	Uses a PC _____	Uses a Mac _____
Has used the computer at a library _____	Has used the World Wide Web for a school project _____	Has used AOL to get on the Internet _____	Has used CompuServe to get on the Internet _____
Talked in a chat room this week _____	Has listened to or downloaded music from the Internet _____	Has used the Internet to find out what books are in the library _____	Has asked a librarian for help on the Internet _____
Has never used the Internet _____	Has received e-mail from someone he or she doesn't know _____	Has been in a private chat room with friends _____	Has used the Internet to check movie times or to compare prices _____

Tangled Communications

Match the terms below with their proper definitions.

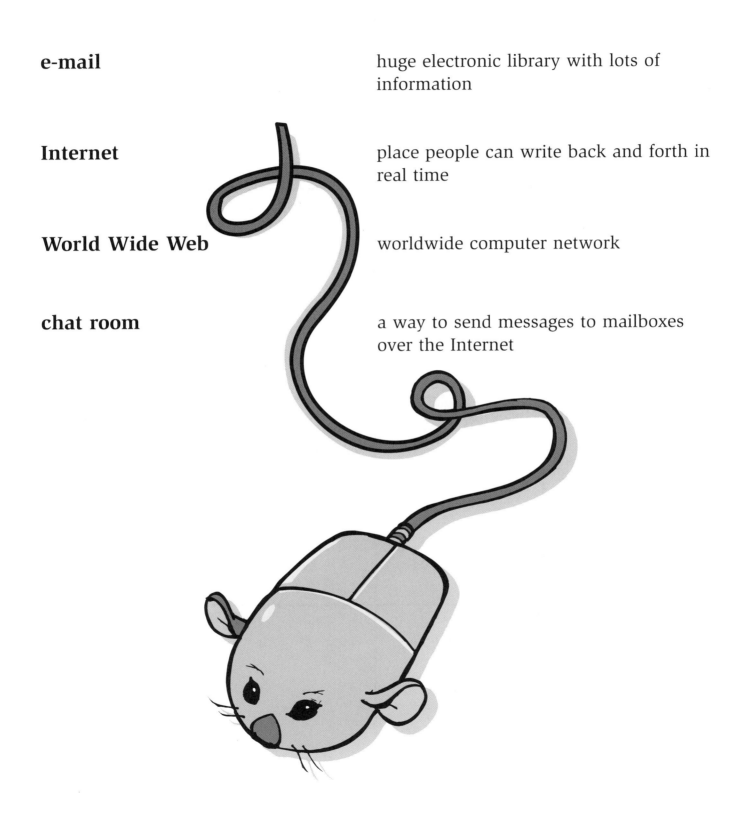

e-mail

huge electronic library with lots of information

Internet

place people can write back and forth in real time

World Wide Web

worldwide computer network

chat room

a way to send messages to mailboxes over the Internet

Name: _____ Date: _____

Internet Systems

Fill in the blanks below with the correct word from the word bank. The words will be used more than once.

---

e-mail • chat room • World Wide Web

Which of the Internet systems listed in the word bank would you most likely use if you wanted to:

- Find recent articles about robots in space? _____

- Have a group discussion about the referee's call at the ice hockey game? _____

- Write to a wildlife rescue center in Australia to find out how they help injured kangaroos? _____

- Find articles about Hinduism? _____

- Contact a veterinarian at the Bronx Zoo to find out how dental care is provided to alligators? _____

- Discuss the president's recent speech with people around the country? _____

The Internet: Who's at the Controls?

Name: _____   Date: _____

The A-maze-ing Message Machine

Allie, Basil, Catherine, Daniel, Eva and Frank are lost! They need to send each other messages to try to find each other again. Can you find a way to send a message from each of them to everyone else? Start at any letter and trace your way through the maze to send a message to each person.

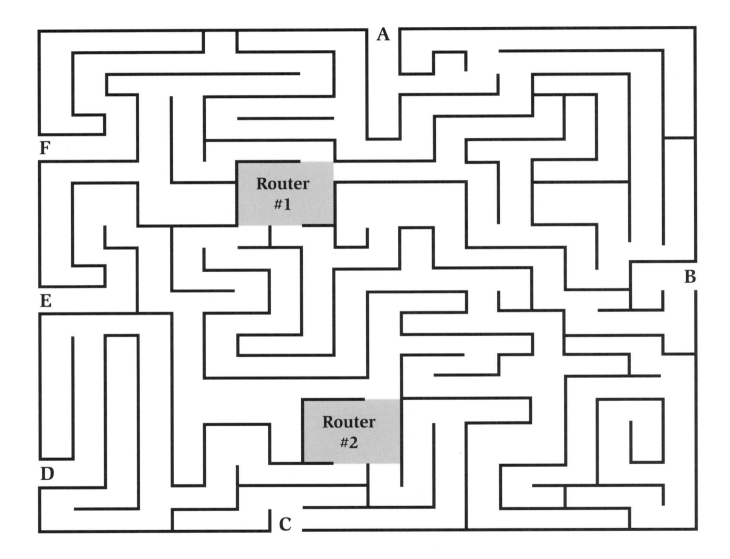

What did you notice about the way each message traveled?

_____

Internet Fact Sheet

The Internet did not begin with the idea that people like us would be using it to send messages back and forth to each other or to surf for information.

The United States Department of Defense started the Internet in the 1960s.

The U.S. Department of Defense wanted to have stronger communication among all its employees who worked in many different places.

Other parts of the government thought the Internet was a good idea, so they started using it, too. The Internet began to grow.

Soon professors and other people who worked at universities started using the Internet to communicate and share their research and ideas.

Finally, by the mid-1990s Internet Service Providers (ISPs) such as AOL were in business. They simplified access to the Internet, making it possible for the rest of the public to gain access.

The Internet is now used by people of all ages throughout the world. It has revolutionized the way the world communicates.

Name: _____   Date: _____

Who's Watching?

Pick the word from under each line that makes the most sense.

Today the Internet is used by _____ of people all over the
hundreds thousands millions

_____. The inventors of the Internet didn't expect it to become
solar system world galaxy

such a huge system, so they did _____ put any plan in place for controlling or
not so too

monitoring information _____ over the Internet. The system just
copied sent believed

keeps getting bigger and bigger, with more and more people using it.

There is an _____ Society (ISOC), which sets standards to help the
Internet Artistic Audubon

Internet run smoothly, _____ no one actually monitors or edits the information
and but then

transmitted over the Internet. There are hundreds of millions of _____
math history Web

pages on the Internet (with thousands being added every day). It would not be

_____ for editors to read and monitor all that information. Even if it
impossible possible kind

were, think how much it would cost to hire them!

Could computers be used in some way to _____ accuracy on the
challenge highlight monitor

Internet? Not yet. They are not sophisticated enough to know the difference between

what is true and what is not, so it is up to users to learn to tell the difference themselves.

Also, monitoring information sent over the Internet would destroy the _____
strength weakness freedom

of the system. However, the price for this freedom is that inaccurate information can be

sent back and forth just as easily as accurate _____. Therefore, it is
information calendars gossip

up to Internet users to be aware of possible problems.

Check Your Memory

ACROSS

1. message(s) sent over the Internet
4. regulate or moderate
7. a worldwide computer network that connects smaller networks
8. review and correct information to get it ready for publication
10. a network that links computers in a local area
11. a discussion area on the Internet where users can communicate in real time
12. a set of computers linked together
14. restriction of information from publication

DOWN

2. false or misleading information
3. a computer that directs information from one computer to another
5. an author's work that has been printed (for example, in a newspaper) or posted or placed on the Internet
6. nickname for the system on the Internet made up of files
9. send
13. a company that provides Internet access

Evaluation Criteria for Web Sites: Domain Names

In this chapter, students will learn about Web site domain names. Emphasis is placed on what the names tell us about Web sites.

Terms Introduced

- browser
- domain
- home page
- hypertext link
- registrar
- Top Level Domain (TLD)
- Universal Resource Locator (URL)
- Web page
- World Wide Web (WWW)

Lesson Plan 1

Web Sites

NET Standards Covered: 1 and 2c

Objectives: Students will be able to:

- learn various uses of the Web
- be able to identify parts of a home page
- become familiar with Web terminology

■ Information Log Activity

Materials:

- Web site that relates to a current topic
- Information Log worksheet (see page 29)

Prepare in Advance:

Assign students the Information Log worksheets to complete as homework before the lesson in class. Make a transparency of a Web site that relates to a current topic. Make a copy for each student.

Directions:

1. In class, ask each student to name two items from the first column on their worksheet. Record the answers on the board.

2. Without writing the headings on the board, group the answers in the following categories: Informational, Persuasive, Promotional (or advertising) and Entertainment.

3. Guide students in using their critical thinking skills to come up with the appropriate category headings. **Note:** The students should also indicate where each type of information would have come from prior to the advent of the Web. The answers do not need to be written on the board, but can be pointed out to emphasize the way Internet use has changed daily life.

4. Ask a volunteer to come up and point out the Web site address on the transparency. Have other volunteers point out the

   - title
   - body copy (text), which describes the scope of the site
   - site links, which show connections to other Web pages within the same site (internal links) or to other sites (external links)

■ Web Terminology Game

Use this game to introduce and reinforce the vocabulary used in this chapter. Students can play as partners or table groups. Have the students race against each other or the clock, to see who can match each word with its definition first. After students become proficient in their knowledge, change the game to memory matching, with all the cards face down in a grid.

Materials:

- Web Race Cards from pages 30–31
- paper cutter or scissors
- laminator or card stock *(optional)*
- envelopes or plastic bags

Prepare in Advance:

Photocopy enough copies of the Web Race Cards for the number of teams you plan to have. Cut the cards apart. If you plan to save the cards from year to year, duplicate them on card stock or laminate them. Mix the cards and store them in envelopes or plastic bags.

Directions:

1. Divide the students into teams. Explain that when you say "go," they are to match the vocabulary cards to their corresponding definitions. The students will already be familiar with some of the words, but other words will require common sense and reasoning skills.

2. Give the teams the go-ahead. If you wish, set a timer for the two teams to race against.

3. Check for accuracy by having two teams compare their answers—one team reads the word card and the other team reads their definition for that word and uses it in a sentence.

4. Discuss the answers as a class, asking students how they arrived at their answers. The game is designed to be played competitively as a race, but should not end until all teams have completed their matches.

Lesson Plan 2

What We Can Learn from Web Addresses

NET Standard Covered: 1a

Objectives: Students will:

- be able to analyze Web addresses and distinguish among commercial, nonprofit, educational, government and military Web sites
- become familiar with the major domain abbreviations for American states and other countries

Time: Approximately 45 minutes

■ Web Address Discussion

1. Write the following URLs on the chalkboard:

   - www.google.com
   - www.redcross.org
   - www.nps.gov
   - www.navy.mil
   - www.harvard.edu

   Ask students to copy the addresses and write what they think they are. Discuss what each of the URLs have in common *(each starts with the letters "www," each has parts separated by periods and each ends with a 3-letter suffix)* and how are they different *(the three letters at the end are different in each URL, the middle section is different in each URL and sometimes the middle section looks like a word).*

2. Tell the students that one of the addresses is for the American Red Cross. Ask a volunteer to identify it and explain how he or she picked it out.

3. Tell them that the other three URLs are addresses for the United States Navy, the National Park Service, a private company that helps people find Web sites and a famous university. Ask students to identify each of the addresses.

4. Introduce the vocabulary word "domain." Explain to students that everything after "www" is called the "domain." Just as we have fingerprints that make each of us unique, every Web site has its own unique domain. The suffix on the far right is called the major domain, or sometimes the top level or first level domain. This part of the address indicates the general type of the Web site.

5. Ask students to infer what type of Web site the following major domains indicate:

   - .org = organization
   - .gov = government
   - .mil = military
   - .edu = education
   - .com = commercial

Be sure to mention that although "gov" is used for most federal and many state domains, sometimes government Web site addresses have different designations. Take, for example, various state departments of education. While California's address is www.cde.ca.gov, Tennessee's is www.state.tn.us/education, Oregon's is www.ode.state.or.us and Mississippi's is www.mde.k12.ms.us. Therefore, while all dot-govs are government sites, not all government sites are listed as dot-govs.

Note: Individuals who have their own Web site, hosted by an Internet service provider or other Web hosting entity, may have more complicated addresses that might include a "~," "member" or "user." Depending on the sophistication of your students, you may or may not include this information in the lesson. Finally, in the same way phone companies add new area codes, new major domain names are being approved as needed to provide more possible Internet addresses.

■ Who's Who on the World Wide Web? Independent Activity

Materials:

- Who's Who on the World Wide Web? worksheets (see page 32)

Directions:

1. Give students a chance to practice deciphering URLs by assigning the Who's Who on the World Wide Web worksheet as independent work.

2. Review the answers together.

■ Major Domain Name Discussion

Inform students that the major domain suffix can be an indicator of a Web site's goals. For instance, a **dot-com** suffix indicates that the site is operated by a commercial enterprise with a product or service to sell, while many **dot-org** suffixes belong to nonprofit, or charitable, organizations that exist to help others, promote ideas or speak out about controversial issues. **Dot-mil** and **dot-gov** suffixes provide information about government agencies and programs; they offer the "official" government point of

view. Educational institutions use **dot-edu** suffixes to pass on information about their schools and programs, as well as to publicize ongoing research done by scholars. All types of sites can provide important and accurate information, but researchers need to be aware that some information may be slanted, skewed or incomplete because it will be influenced by the sponsor's goals. This activity will help students identify the slant of the information they might find on fictitious Web sites so that they will begin to become aware of sources of bias in their independent research on the web.

■ Keep Your Eyes on the Goal Activity

Materials:

- Keep Your Eyes on the Goal! worksheet (see page 33)

Directions:

1. Assign the worksheet as individual or partner work.

2. Correct the assignment together, reinforcing the manner in which the goals of each question are best served by the goal of a Web site. Remind students that the major domain gives an indication of the sponsor's purpose. For example, question 2 asks for a donation, which will most likely be supplied by the "preserve our music" dot-org. The place to locate a military band will probably be at "usnavy" dot-mil, and a dot-gov suffix will be part of the local library's URL. **Note:** All Web sites mentioned in this activity are intended to be fictional. Due to the constantly changing nature of the Internet, some URLs may be in actual use.

■ World Wide Web Codes Discussion

Explain that the URLs studied so far are addresses for World Wide Web sites in the United States. Since the World Wide Web encompasses the whole world, there are special addresses to get to sites in other countries. URLs for other countries usually end in a two-letter country code. Even some addresses in the United States end in a two-letter country code.

There are also two-letter codes for the 50 states in the United States. Write this address on the board as an example, and ask students what they think the last two parts stand for: www.vcss.k12.ca.us.

Explain that this is the address of the Ventura County Superintendent of Schools Office in California. Ask: Which part stands for California? Which part stands for the United States?

It's important to know abbreviations when doing research. That way, you are sure to get the information you want. For example, typing "Portland" on your search line could take you to Maine or Oregon, but knowing the abbreviations for those states (ME and OR) will help you get to the links you need when writing your state report.

When state abbreviations are used on the Internet, they are almost always the same as the standard two-letter postal abbreviations. You can find a list of the abbreviations by typing "state abbreviations" in the search line and following one of the many links provided.

Chapter Review

Materials:

- Chapter 2 Review worksheet (see page 34)

Directions:

1. Have students complete the Chapter Review on page 34 to test their comprehension. The worksheet can be completed in class or as homework.

2. Check the answers as a class.

Key Concepts in Chapter 2

- The World Wide Web (WWW) is the part of the Internet most heavily used for research.

- The most common purposes of Web sites are to inform, persuade, promote (advertise) and entertain.

- A Web site has links that can take the user to other Web pages within the same site (internal links) or pages at other Web sites (external links).

- The Universal Resource Locator (URL) tells us the address of a Web site.

- The Top Level Domain (TLD) is represented by the URL's ending letters. It indicates the type of Web site. Some of the most common TLD's are:

    .edu (colleges and universities)

    .com (business)

    .gov (government)

    .org (organization)

    .mil (military)

- The type and purpose of the site may suggest the need for further research to verify accuracy of information.

Name: _____   Date: _____

Information Log

Survey people you know to find out what information they looked for this week on the Internet. Ask them where they would have looked for the same information before the Internet existed. Record their answers on this log.

Information searched for:	Where I would have found it before the Internet existed:
1.	
2.	
3.	
4.	

Web Race Cards

The Web	A huge collection of electronic pages filled with written information, graphics, sound and video clips.
Web Site	One or more Web pages belonging to an individual, group or organization.
Home Page	The main page of a Web site. It usually has an index telling what is contained on the site.
Hypertext Links	Highlighted words or graphics found on Web pages. A user can jump to a new page on the Web site by clicking on the link. Sometimes they even take you to a new Web site altogether!
Server (Web Server)	A special kind of software program that stores Web pages, then provides them to computers that request the information.

Web Race Cards (continued)

Web Browser	Software program that allows a user to connect to a Web server. The most common ones are Microsoft® Internet Explorer, Netscape® and Netscape Navigator.
Registrar	A company that a person or organization pays to register their unique Web address so that no one else can use it.
Domain Name	The part of a web address that follows the "www."
URL	The Universal Resource Locator, a fancy name for a Web site address.
Search Engine	A program used to search for information on the World Wide Web. *www.google.com* is a popular one.

Who's Who on the World Wide Web

Match the companies, schools, organizations, government agencies and military groups on the left with their Web site addresses (URLs) on the right.

Pomona College   www.af.mil

American Red Cross   www.federalreserve.gov

Ford Motor Company   www.walmart.com

World Wildlife Fund   www.senate.gov

United States Senate   www.petsmart.com

Petsmart   www.soccer.org

Washington State University   www.schwinn.com

Federal Reserve Board   www.aspca.org

AYSO   www.Pomona.edu

United States Air Force   www.redcross.org

Schwinn Bicycles   www.panda.org

Wal-Mart   www.Ford.com

American Society for the Prevention   www.wsu.edu
of Cruelty to Animals

Keep Your Eyes on the Goal

Ms. Sweetwater's fifth grade class is planning their booth for the school carnival. They decide that they want to create a game based on the American Revolution, and that they will also sell desserts and candies that were eaten by children who lived in the 1700s. Austin, Marina and Joe volunteered to find out more about these topics on the Internet. Can you help them out? Be sure to think about the **goal** of each question and match it with the Web site that will probably have a similar goal. Write the letter of the correct Web site above the correct question number at the bottom of the page.

Question	Web Site	
1. What were the names of the 5 biggest battles?	www.nationallibrary.gov	**A**
2. Is there a group that will lend us CDs of patriotic music?	www.geographyclass.edu	**I**
3. Did Paul Revere really ride through Boston on a horse?	www.amerrevolutioncollege.edu	**H**
4. Is there a military band that can come play at the carnival?	www.oldtymestore.com	**I**
5. How many soldiers fought in the war?	www.preserveourmusic.org	**O**
6. When did the first battle start?	www.flagsflagsflags.com	**Y**
7. Who will sell us inexpensive battle maps to use for the games?	www.reveremonument.gov	**P**
8. Where can we buy replicas of the first American flag?	www.revolutionarytimeline.edu	**O**
9. Where is Bunker Hill?	www.rememberthesoldiers.org	**H**
10. Where can we buy the old-fashioned ingredients for the candy?	www.historicmaps.com	**H**
11. What kind of candy was made in the colonies?	www.usmilitarybands.mil	**P**
12. Are there any cookbooks at the local library with authentic colonial recipes?	www.historiccookingschool.edu	**R**

"___ ___ ___, ___ ___ ___, ___ ___ ___ ___ ___ ___, **you helped save the day!**"
     1   9   4   7   10   3   5   2   6   11   12   8

Name: _____   Date: _____

Chapter 2 Review

Fill in the blanks using words from the word bank.

1. Nickname for "www." _____ _____

2. Set of Web pages belonging to a person or organization. _____ _____

3. Abbreviation for the technical name used to mean "Web site address." _____

4. Highlighted word or picture on a Web page that takes the user to another Web page. _____ _____

5. Main page of a Web site, which usually has links to other sites. _____ _____

6. Part of a Web site address. _____ _____

7. The organization or company that users pay to have their Web sites entered onto the Internet. _____

8. A special computer that provides a service, such as e-mail or Web information, to other computers. _____

9. A program that allows a user to read information on the Web. _____

10. A program used to search for information on the Web. _____ _____

Word Bank			
domain name	home page	the Web	hypertext link
registrar	server	browser	search engine
URL	Web site		

3 Evaluation Criteria for Web Sites: Authority

The Web is by far the largest area of the Internet used for research. Although most of the information is accurate and well-written, there is a great deal that is not. This chapter discusses criteria for evaluating an author and a Web site.

Terms Introduced

- authority
- expert
- expertise
- home page
- professions
- sponsor

Lesson Plan 1

Identifying an Author and Locating Information About an Author

NET Standard Covered: 5a and 5c

Objectives: Students will be able to:

- locate the author of a Web site
- locate information about the author

■ Discussion

The Internet can be likened to a newspaper. It changes daily and the authors of every article are not clearly identified. This lesson teaches students how to locate the author's name and information on Internet Web sites.

Unlike books, where the author is clearly identified on the title page, an Internet author can publish a Web site without identifying who he or she is. Many authors do identify themselves and give their credentials, but they are not always found on the Web page that a student is referred to by a key word search.

When students search for information with a search engine like Yahoo Kids or Google, the engine connects them directly to the page within a Web site that contains the key words. In many cases, this is not the Web site's home page. In order to identify the author of an article, many authors include personal information and claims of expertise on the home page of their Web sites. Others devote an entire page to providing this information, and even include e-mail links so that readers can contact them directly.

Some types of sites, such as government agencies and large non-profit groups, do not usually identify the author of specific articles. They rely on their reputations to substantiate the information they provide.

Before asking students to look for author information independently, be sure that they are familiar with the concept of a home page. If your school has its own Web site, with links to teachers and classrooms, it can be used as an example of how to navigate through the Web pages on any Web site. If your school does not have a Web site yet, you might use www.TeacherWeb.com as a resource. It has links to schools in all parts of the country, and you can locate a school near you or one in an area you are studying.

■ Author Activity

Materials:

- Who's the Author? worksheet for each student or pair of students (see page 40)
- Flow Chart for each student or pair of students (see page 41)

- overhead transparency of Who's the Author? worksheet and Flow Chart for classroom discussion

- computers for small group/partner exploration

- chalkboard or chart paper to record results of discussion

Directions:

1. In this activity, students will locate five different Web sites about a single subject. They will visit each Web site and try to locate the author's name and information about the author. Have them record their findings on the Who's the Author? worksheet.

2. Students may work individually, with a partner or in a small group, depending on the number of computers available for the exploration.

3. At the end of the exploration, hold a class discussion and decide which kinds of Web sites usually contained information about the author. Students should conclude that government and large non-profit groups or corporations often do not include author information, whereas sites sponsored by individuals and small groups usually do.

Lesson Plan 2

Credentials and Expertise

NET Standards Covered: 2a and 5c

Objectives: Students will be able to:

- understand the concept of expertise

- become familiar with selected career credentials and levels of college degrees

■ Discussion

Ask the class to define "expert" and write all reasonable answers on the board. The final answer should include the concept of having special knowledge or skills. Point out that "authority" is often used as a synonym for "expert."

Have the students form small groups of 3–5 students. Write the following words on the board:

car mechanic	river raft guide
doctor	teacher
parachutist	lawyer

Ask students to discuss among themselves how people develop expertise in the above areas. Have them write down their ideas. Then focus on one area at a time and ask a spokesperson from each group to present ideas to the class. Guide students to realize that some areas of expertise are developed through training and education while others are gained solely through experience.

■ Expertise Activity

Materials:

- Levels of Training and Education guidelines (see page 42)

- Expertise Activity worksheet (see page 43)

- WinnerInternet Activity (see page 44)

Directions:

1. Pass out the guidelines that define the levels of training and professional degrees.

2. Ask the students to note that not all of the initials after names refer to the types of educational degrees a person has earned. Some describe the person's career training. For example, a registered nurse has the initials R.N. Some people have more than one set of initials after their names, showing that they have completed multiple training programs. For example, an orthodontist has earned a D.D.S. degree as well as an M.S. (master of science) in orthodontic studies.

3. Have the students complete the Expertise Activity and the WinnerInternet Activity. These can be done in class or as homework.

4. Review the answers together.

Lesson Plan 3

Identifying the Authority of a Web Site (Sponsor) and Locating Information About the Sponsor

NET Standards Covered: 5 and 6

Objectives: Students will be able to:

- identify sponsorship of sites

- locate official sites of dot-coms, dot-orgs, dot-edus and dot-govs

- tell the difference between official sites and sites with similar addresses

■ Discussion

When you listen to the radio or watch TV, have you ever wondered who pays for the shows? Most shows are paid for or sponsored by advertisers (the ones whose ads are aired during station breaks). Web sites need money to stay on the Internet, too. How do you think they are sponsored, that is, who pays for the sites?

The answer to that question is usually found in the major domain names. Dot-govs are sponsored by government agencies, dot-orgs are generally paid for by the organizations featured in the site, dot-coms by the companies advertised on the site and dot-edus by the schools they represent. When you are doing a search, you have to be careful to look closely at Web addresses. They can be very similar, and some-

times the similarities are misleading. For example, if you are researching information on the Internal Revenue Service, you will find many sites, but only ones with www.irs.gov in their addresses are official government sites. Others, which may contain information about the IRS, may provide useful information as well, but just keep in mind that the purposes of the various domains are very different. For example, dot-govs generally provide free services to the public, but dot-coms sell products or services.

Another problem is that some sites might sound legitimate, but are actually money-making hoaxes. (See chapter 7 for more information on hoaxes.) Just because an address has the domain letters "org" in its address, it doesn't mean that the organization is reputable. Remember that, for the most part, the Internet is not monitored when it comes to dot-orgs and dot-coms, and anyone can post a site in these domains. For example, the site www.cancer cure.org sounds good, right? Who wouldn't want to contribute to it? But if such a Web site existed, which it does not at the writing of this book, it could be a hoax or scam. A good rule is that if you come across an organization with which you are not familiar, check it out further. First do a Web search and see if there are any other references to it on sites you can trust. If not, you can ask your local librarian to help you research it. She has powerful online resources she can use, as well as reference books that contain information about organizations.

■ Computer Lab Activity

Materials:

- computer lab with online access (or chalkboard for alternate activity)

Directions:

1. Divide the students into small groups and assign each group one or two organizations/agencies/companies/schools from the list on page 38.

2. The students' task is to locate the official Web sites for each of them. If students find other similar looking Web site addresses, they should note them; the differences between the official Web sites and the similar ones can be discussed in class if time permits. Indicate to the class that sometimes

the words "official site" or "corporate site" may be indicated next to the Web site address. However, sometimes a site is official even though those words don't appear. Students need to use their common sense in recognizing official sites. Also remember that there are exceptions to the rules, and while most sites that say they are "official" truly are, occasionally a site will indicate that it is official (especially for a dot-com), when in fact it is not. Therefore, if you have any doubts about a site's authenticity, it is a good idea to read its material carefully and check multiple sources to be sure you are getting what you intended.

Note: Answers are listed in parentheses.

- Make a Wish Foundation *(www.wish.org)*

- The Cubs (baseball team) *(www.cubs.com)*

- California State Department of Motor Vehicles *(www.dmv.ca.gov)*

- DCShoe *(www.dcshoe.com)*

- Braille Institute of America *(www.brailleinstitute.org)*

- United States Food and Drug Administration *(www.fda.gov)*

- Willamette University *(www.willamette.edu)*

- United Cerebral Palsy *(www.ucp.org)*

- Boston Bruins (hockey team) *(www.bostonbruins.com)*

- University of Wisconsin—Madison *(www.wisc.edu)*

- United States Senate *(www.senate.gov)*

- Firestone Tires *(www.firestone.com)*

- New York University *(www.nyu.edu)*

- Boy Scouts of America *(www.scouting.org)*

- Procter and Gamble *(www.pg.com)*

- Veterans of Foreign Wars *(www.vfw.org)*

Alternate Activity:

If access to computers is not available at the time of the activity, write several of the above schools, companies and agencies in a column on a chalk board. Next to the names, write either the official Web site address **or** a made up address that looks somewhat similar, but either has a different major domain at the end (such as "gov" instead of "com") or is changed in some other way. See if the students can identify which are official sites and which are not, and have them give their reasoning.

Pop-up Ads

Often there are pop-up ads that appear during searches that have nothing to do with the sites you are exploring or their sponsors. Sometimes it's hard to tell what belongs to a site and what doesn't, since many sites have sidebars, flashing graphics or links that can be confused with ads from outside sources. Discuss pop-up ads with your students.

Key Concepts in Chapter 3

When evaluating Web site articles, check to see if:

- You can identify the author of a Web site and information about him or her.

- The authors have expertise (appropriate education or experience) in the area on which they are writing.

- You can identify the sponsor of a Web site and information about the sponsor.

- The Web site's grammar and spelling are accurate.

Who's the Author?

Finding an author's name on a Web site is not always as easy as it is in a book. In fact, sometimes it seems like the author doesn't want you to know his or her name. In other cases, if you are a good detective and follow the clues on the Web site, you will find the author's name along with other information about him or her. The author might share the reasons he or she created the Web site, or maybe even post a picture of his or her dog!

Choose a topic that interests you, such as:

- your favorite sport or hobby, such as soccer or stamp collecting

- an animal you are interested in, such as sea turtles or sharks

- your favorite author or a place you would like to visit

- something you are studying in school

Use a search engine like Google or Yahoo Kids, and visit at least five Web sites about your topic. Try to pick Web sites with different domain addresses (.gov, .com, .org). Follow the flow chart to look for author information. Record the WWW address and the author information on the table below. Be ready to talk about it with the rest of your class!

Our topic was: _____

	Web Address	Name of Article	Author's Name	Author Information/ Contact Information
1.				
2.				
3.				
4.				
5.				

Flow Chart

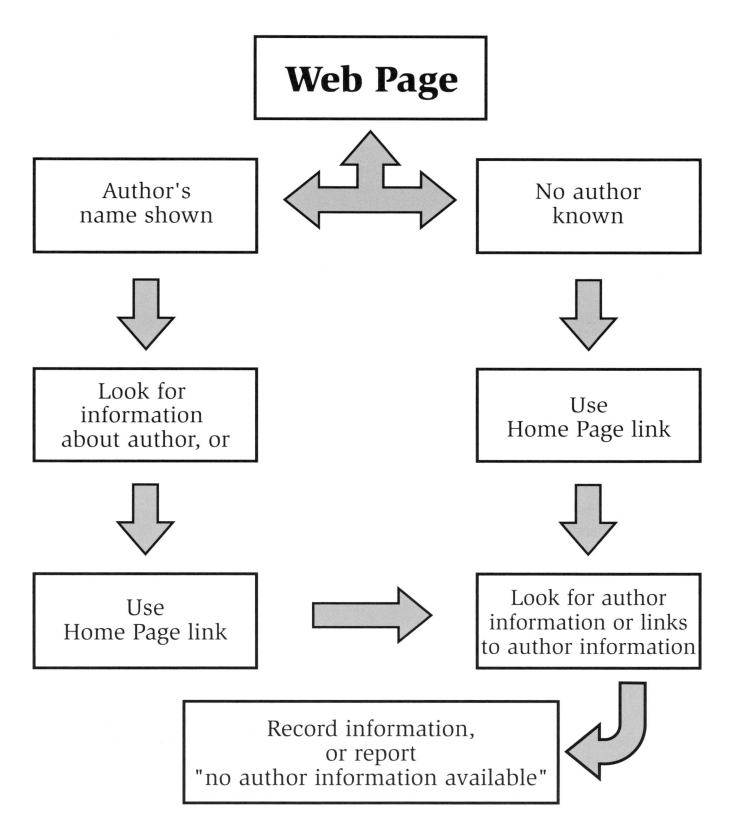

Web Page

Author's name shown

No author known

Look for information about author, or

Use Home Page link

Use Home Page link

Look for author information or links to author information

Record information, or report "no author information available"

Evaluation Criteria for Web Sites: Authority   **41**

Levels of Training and Education Guidelines

Certificate: Can be earned at a college or trade school for many types of technical or hands-on programs. Examples include car mechanics, welding, business computer operations, certified nursing assistant, dental technician and chef.

Degrees: Earned at colleges and universities for academic areas. Examples include English, math and history.

- Associate of Arts (AA) or Associate of Science (AS): 2-year programs offered at community colleges

- Bachelor of Arts (BA or AB) or Bachelor of Science (BS): 4-year programs offered at colleges and universities

- Master of Arts (MA) or Master of Science (MS): 1–2 year programs offered at graduate schools

- Doctor of Philosophy (PhD—also called a "doctorate"): 4–5 year program beyond bachelor's degree or 2–3 year programs following master's degree. Offered at graduate schools. Note: This degree is not really related to the study of philosophy. A PhD can be earned in most fields, including math and science and means that a person not only has extensive knowledge in the field, but has also completed significant research in the area.

Examples of Professional Abbreviations

Arts Professions

- B Arch—Bachelor of Arts in Architecture
- MFA—Master of Fine Arts

Engineering Professions

- CE—Civil Engineer
- ME—Mechanical Engineer

Legal Professions

- JD or LLD—lawyer (3 years of law school)

Medical Professions

- MD—Medical Doctor (4 years college, 4 years medical school, minimum 3 additional training)
- RN—Registered Nurse (3 or more years of training)
- LVN—Licensed Vocational Nurse (one year of training)
- DDS or DMD—Dentist
- DVM—Veterinarian

Religious Professions

- MDiv—Master's Degree
- ThD—Doctor of Theology

Social Work and Counseling Professions

- MSW—Master of Social Work
- MFCC—Marriage and Family Counselor
- MFT—Marriage and Family Therapist
- PhD Psych—Psychologist with doctorate

Tip
Confused about an abbreviation? Find out what it means by going to: **www.acronymfinder.com**

Name: _____ Date: _____

Expertise Activity

The following articles and authors are fictitious. Write the letters for the professional degrees that would follow their names on the blank lines.

1. "Flossing for Fun" by Moe Larr, _____.

2. "Working for a Doctor" by Lotta Shottzy, _____ (or _____).

3. "How to Medically Treat Skunks" by Vair E. Kairfull, _____.

4. "My Life as a Surgeon" by N. O. Bonaparte, _____.

5. "Emerging Religions in Transylvania" Dr. A. Cula, _____.

6. "Mechanical Advances in Automobile Engines" by V. Roome, _____.

7. "How Road Repairs Affect Safe Speed Limits" by Fess Terwego, _____.

8. "The Benefits of Marriage Counseling" by Liz N. Tuyu, _____.

9. "Obey or Pay: Consequences for Law Breakers" by Judd G. Meante, _____.

10. "Religions of the Ancient World" by Manny I. Dols, _____.

11. "How to Design Your Own Patio" by Archie Tecker, _____.

WinnerInternet Activity

The following people have published articles on the WinnerInternet. Which one should you believe? Remember to check out their credentials! Circle the article that you think would have the most reliable information.

1. "The Anatomy of a Horse" by Dr. Barnstable, DVM.

   "Horse Diseases" by Dr. Haymore, MD.

2. "Why We Need Laws" by I. M. Kopp, MSW.

   "Crime and its Consequences" by John Doe, LLD.

3. "Native American Religious Traditions Before Columbus" by Abe Smith, MDiv.

   "The Hindu Religion in India" by Ellen Fanta, LVN.

4. "How to Get Along with Your Father" by Myson Allen, MFCC

   "Kids Should Love Their Parents" by G. Rand, MA.

5. "Bridge-Building for Kids" by Ernest Lee, JD.

   "How to Build Your Own Log Cabin" by Monty Mann, B Arch.

Extra Challenge: Make up two articles of your own!

_____

_____

Evaluation Criteria for Web Sites: Currency

In an age characterized by rapid exchange of information as well as constant advances in technology, facts can quickly become out of date. This chapter helps develop critical thinking skills that students need to decide when currency (and recency) of material affect the accuracy and value of information located on the Internet.

Terms Introduced

- currency
- recency
- relative
- historical

Lesson Plan 1

Currency, Sources and Presentation

NET Standards Covered: 2a, 2c, 5c and 6

Objectives: Students will be able to:

- decide when currency is important to a Web site

- check to make sure that the author lists sources that can be verified

- look at grammar and spelling to see if the article was written carefully

■ Discussion

Review the meaning of the word "current," pointing out that currency, as used in this chapter, is simply the noun form. Also, discuss the word "recent." Talk about the fact that recent (and its noun derivative "recency") relate to a relative concept. You may want to illustrate with an example such as the following:

A discovery of dinosaur bones 10 years ago would likely be considered a recent discovery, when considering how long ago dinosaurs lived and how infrequently we make new discoveries about them. However, an invention from 10 years ago in the area of computers might not be considered recent, since computers are relatively new, and there are so many advances each year.

■ Web Site Reliability Activity

Materials:

- chalk board

Time: 15 minutes

Directions:

1. Read the following article title to students: "Latest Advances in Snowboard Design." Ask if it sounds like a reasonable source to use for a report on state-of-the-art snowboards. After a show of hands, tell the students the article was written in 1995. Ask if they still think it would be a good article to use. Reinforce the fact that it is very important to check the date of the article, as the information, once current, could now be out of date.

2. Divide students into groups of three or four each. Write the following fictional Web site articles on the board. Give students up to 10 minutes to discuss the titles in their groups and decide whether "currency" is important to the accuracy of the articles.

   - "How Thomas Edison Changed His World"

   - "Recent Advances in Medicine"

   - "What We Know about Mars"

- "Battles of World War II"
- "Raising Your Pet Hamster"
- "Today's Weather"
- "Cesar Chavez's Contributions to History"
- "Cartoons of the 1950s"
- "Baseball Records"
- "Germany Today"

3. Review the answers together.

4. Advise students that it is important to look at Web sites to see when they were last updated, reminding them that Web site authors/sponsors don't always bother to take outdated information off the Web. Ask if any students know where to look on a Web site to see when a site was first created and/or last updated. If computer access is available in the classroom, bring up some sites and let them find the answer. If not, let them know that dates, when listed, are usually listed on the home page of a site, at the top or bottom of the page.

5. If an article is time-sensitive, such as some of the fictional articles above, and a date is not shown on a Web site, ask students what they should do, guiding them to realize that further research would be necessary to verify how current the information is.

6. Note that although some articles may be outdated, they can be of use when tracking changes over time. For example, if a student is doing a report on Mars, he or she may want to read an article on "What We Know about Mars" from 1995 and compare it to more recent information in order to show recent advances in technology and knowledge.

Three Notable Problems Arise When Checking Currency

Discuss these currency issues with your students.

- Authors or Web site sponsors often forget (or get lazy) and don't take their outdated materials off the Internet.

- Sometimes there are no dates to indicate when articles were written and/or when the information was last updated.

- Sometimes an article, while current itself, may be linked to other sites that are not up to date.

For these reasons, information that is questionably current, should be verified by other reliable sources. See Chapter 5.

Key Concepts in Chapter 4

When evaluating Web site articles, check to see if:

- The information is up to date.

- The authors have listed the sources so that you can verify the information.

- The Web site's links are current.

Evaluation Criteria for the Internet: Verifiability

Verifying information is an important research skill, whether the information is gleaned from the Internet or from print, television or radio sources. The Internet poses special challenges because its open nature allows anyone to post information. For these reasons, students must learn to document their sources and to confirm information by using a variety of media in their research projects. This chapter will utilize lab exercises, discussion activities and a game to help students recognize the need to verify information they find on the Internet.

Note: Hoaxes, scams and other forms of "netlore," while occasionally found in Web sites, are more abundant in e-mail. They are featured in Chapter 7.

Terms Introduced

- context
- headers
- original source
- paraphrase
- perspective
- reliable
- verify
- webliography

Lesson Plan

Verifying Information and Checking Original Sources

NET Standards Covered: 5 and 6

Objectives: Students will be able to:

- decide which information needs verifying
- locate original sources in order to check out questionable information
- identify reliable sources to use for verification

■ Warm-up Game

Time: Approximately 10 minutes

Directions:

1. Play telephone. Have the class stand or sit in a circle. You can join them. Start a message of your choice around the circle by whispering it to the person to your right, and have him or her whisper the message as he or she heard it to the person to the right. Continue until the message has gone around the circle.

2. Have the last person say the message aloud to the class. Compare it with the original message you started. (Almost always the passed message will end up significantly different than the original.)

■ Discussion

Have the class talk about the process that occurred when the message went from one person to another. Point out that when people hear facts, they often remember only what seems important to them. They may also slant the information to fit their perspective. For this reason it is important to check with the original source, that is, the person the information originated with. When you do this you are verifying the truth and reliability of the information.

Ask students what reliable sources they could use to verify a rumor that a robbery had occurred on their street. Possible answers might include checking with the family that was robbed, calling the police department for information, checking a local newspaper, etc. Ask if information from another neighbor would be considered reliable. Why or why not?

Ask students what should make them question material they read. What should make them decide that it needs to be verified? Their answers should include: the information seems ridiculous or unreasonable based on what they already know; the source of the information is not well known or has a poor reputation; and the information is on a controversial topic.

■ Brainstorming Activity

Materials:

- Wild Claims Cards cut apart to distribute to groups (see page 52)
- 4–5 large index cards per group of students
- pocket chart or tape

Time: 10–15 minutes

Directions:

1. Divide the class into groups of four or five and give each group one or two of the Wild Claims Cards and four large index cards.

2. Ask students to brainstorm how they could verify whether the information on their Wild Claims Cards is true. They should use the index cards to record their ideas—one idea per card.

3. After students have had time to work with their team, have them read their amazing fact out loud, and then tell at least three ways they would try to verify it.

4. Collect the index cards after each group has reported. Review by sorting the index cards into categories using the pocket chart or taping them to a large piece of chart paper. Summarize by pointing out that information can be verified in many ways, including:

   - consulting encyclopedias, almanacs and dictionaries
   - asking an expert
   - looking in books on the subject
   - using newspapers
   - asking the reference librarian for help

■ Discussion

Keep the students in the small groups from the previous activity. Remind them that sometimes they may get information through e-mail or in a chat room, as well as from Internet articles. Have them write down ideas on how to locate original sources for information learned from these three areas.

Many times authors will paraphrase (summarize briefly in their own words) a fact they have heard or read, but they may misrepresent or use the fact differently than it was intended. Another problem is that they may use it out of context, that is, without supplying other information that puts the proper perspective on the fact. For this reason, it is extremely important to check questionable facts with original sources.

As a class, discuss answers, which may include the following:

E-mail: Checking the headers (information in small print at the bottom of the e-mail) that shows the trail of addresses through which the e-mail has been forwarded. Look to see where the e-mail originated.

Chat rooms: Asking the person who sent you the e-mail specifically where he or she got his or her information.

Web articles: Look at the bibliography, if one is included. Go back to those sources to check out information, if possible. If it's a webliography source (source from the Web), it should be easy to find if the site still exists. If it doesn't exist anymore, check out other sources to confirm your information.

Reliable Sources: Ask students where they can go to find reliable information if they cannot find the original source, or if they do find it but doubt the accuracy of its information. Write all reasonable answers on the board, which may include articles from dot-edu sources, dot-govs or dot-orgs representing organizations of long standing with good reputations such as the American Red Cross, American Cancer Society, etc. Then ask your students who can help them identify reliable sources. Answers may include teachers, parents and librarians. Ask them what sources they can trust. Encyclopedias, almanacs and other books in the reference section of the library are excellent resources to use in verifying information. (Some of these references can be found online as well.)

Follow-up:

Take students to the computer lab and library so they can verify the information on their Wild Claims cards.

Libraries

Librarians are trained to evaluate the accuracy and reliability of information found on the Internet as well as in books, magazines, etc. Many librarians recommend Web sites by placing links to sites that provide quality information on a variety of subjects on their home page.

Libraries also subscribe to specialized databases or Web sites that often are too expensive for the average person to afford on their own. Generally, patrons of the library can access these databases free of charge through the library's home page. The library selects databases that provide quality information on topics of importance to patrons.

The librarian can help the public verify information found on the Internet through a number of ways. First, he or she can help research the qualifications of the author who is writing on the particular subject. Next, the librarian can confirm the accuracy of a particular Web site by finding a second source for the same information. Lastly, the librarian can help determine whether the information is the most current that is available.

(Information provided by Beth Walker, Reference Librarian, Pasadena (CA) Public Library.)

Key Concepts in Chapter 5

- Information from the Internet should be verified when it:
  - does not seem logical based on what you already know
  - comes from an author whose expertise is not known or who has a poor reputation
  - is controversial in nature

- When verifying questionable information from the Web, it is best to check with its original source or to confirm the information with another source you know to be reliable.

- Librarians can direct you to reputable Web sites or books and magazines you can use to verify questionable information.

Wild Claims Cards

Copy and cut apart. Distribute one or two facts to each brainstorming group.

About 20 billion disposable diapers are buried in U.S. landfills each year. They take about 500 years to decompose!	Penguins build their nests out of rocks.	Winds produced by tornadoes can blow at over 300 miles per hour.
The world's longest street is over 1,100 miles long!	There are more than 10,000 varieties of tomatoes.	The average life of a major league baseball is five to seven pitches.
Saffron, a spice made from flowers, costs more than $3000 a pound!	The average North American teenager drinks more than six glasses of soda every day.	Babies are born with 300 bones, but by the time they grow up they only have 206!
More soldiers died of disease during the American Civil War than died on the battlefield.	A heat wave in Europe in the summer of 2003 killed more than 35,000 people.	Elephants can make sounds heard 50 miles away.

Evaluation Criteria for Web Sites: Bias

This chapter deals with the information quality of a Web site. It focuses on content and information, and gives students practice recognizing the differences between fact and opinion. There are three guided explorations that allow students to apply their learning to real research situations. Next, the chapter includes an independent project especially suited to the differentiated instruction required for Gifted and Talented students. It concludes with guidelines for evaluating Web sites and tips for developing sound sites.

Terms Introduced

- bias
- fact
- opinion
- point of view

Lesson Plan 1

Bias: The Whole Truth

When students begin to use the Internet for research, they tend to believe that all information they find is true and complete. This lesson will help students realize that the Internet is a form of media similar to magazines, newspapers and television. As such, it often contains information that is inaccurate or that doesn't tell the whole story. This lesson will focus on the effects of incomplete information, i.e., the difference between the truth and the whole truth.

NET Standards Covered: 2

Objectives: Students will be able to:

- understand the effects of withholding part of the truth
- realize they will encounter partial truths on the Internet in sites intended to promote products or ideas

■ The Real Truth Activity

Materials:

- one copy per student of "The Real Truth About Humpty Dumpty" (see pages 59–60)

Time: 30 minutes

Directions:

1. Write the following sentence on the board: "Do you swear to tell the truth, the __ __ __ __ __ truth, and nothing but the truth?" Ask students where they have heard that question before. If they are not familiar with it, explain that it is part of the oath a person takes prior to testifying in court. Ask them to fill in the missing word, and discuss why the word "whole" is so important to the concept of truth.

2. Illustrate the point of the lesson by passing out the script. Have students take turns reading the script, or have a group of students perform the script.

3. Discuss whether any of the witnesses lied at any time or if any of them did not tell the whole truth.

■ Additional Activity

Alternatively, discuss the following scenarios:

1. Mr. Jones is accused of dumping toxic waste in an unlawful area last winter. He testifies in court that he could not have done so because he was out of town the day the waste was dumped. Later it is discovered that he was in fact out of town that day, but had paid someone else to dump the waste for him. Did he actually lie? Did he tell the whole truth?

2. Promo-pops is a company that makes frozen bars. It advertises its product as being made from real fruit juice. Assuming the company's claim is true, can you be sure just from the ad that the frozen bars are good for you?

Why or why not? Does the ad say how much of the frozen bars are made from real fruit? Does it say what other ingredients (such as sugar) are added? Is the Promo-pops company lying in its ad? Is it telling the whole truth?

Students should realize that when looking at ads or reading articles on the Internet, sometimes it is as important to think about what is not being said as much as what is.

Lesson Plan 2

Evaluating Bias in the Media

This lesson focuses on issues related to partial truths. It will help students recognize other forms of bias, with particular attention to differentiating between fact and opinion. Understanding some of the reasons that bias exists will help students identify it when they are using Internet sources. **Note:** Many schools require students to receive drug, alcohol and tobacco use prevention education. This lesson is very effective using advertisements for these products to teach media awareness.

NET Standards Covered: 2

Objectives: Students will be able to:

- understand the concept of bias

- analyze print media for evidence of bias

■ The Octopus Skateboard Activity

Materials:

- overhead transparency of the Octopus Skateboard worksheet and enough copies for each pair of students (see page 61)

- Media Analysis worksheet for each student (see page 62)

- 3" x 5" index card per student

- dark markers

- dictionaries

Directions:

1. Ask students what the difference is between fact and opinion. Allow them about three minutes to write down their answer to the question.

2. Have partners or table groups share their answers with each other, asking them to try to choose one person from their group who has the most complete answer to share with the whole class.

3. Write the word "bias" on the board and give students one minute to look up its many meanings in the dictionary. Challenge them to find a meaning that could relate to facts and opinions. Call on volunteers to read the parts of the definition that they believe apply. Record major points on the board under the word "bias." Establish the idea that bias means that information is slanted so that it supports someone's opinion or point of view, while facts are objective evidence of happenings or characteristics of products.

4. Pass out the index cards and dark markers. Ask students to write the word "fact" on one side and "opinion" on the other side.

5. Put the Octopus Skateboard transparency on the overhead. Tell students that this is an advertisement for a new invention that might be sold to children their ages. As you have volunteers read portions of the advertisement, ask the class to hold up their index cards to indicate whether the portion read is a fact or an opinion. Survey the cards as they are held up and stop to clarify uncertainties or misunderstandings as necessary.

6. Pass out one copy of the Octopus Skateboard worksheet for each pair of students, as well as a copy of the Media Analysis worksheet for each student. Ask them to look at the ad with their partners and to find information that matches the major areas on their analysis sheet.

7. Allow a few minutes for students to jot down their ideas in the appropriate spaces on the analysis worksheet. Then begin a class discussion.

■ Discussion

Discuss the Octopus Skateboard ad by asking the following questions. The anticipated responses are in italics.

- What product is being sold? *skateboard*

- What special features does the skateboard have? *8 wheels, x-shaped board, swiveling wheels*

- What promises does the manufacturer make in words? *You'll do new tricks, have freedom, go faster, set world records, own something rare and expensive.*

- Does the manufacturer make any other promises? What are they? How does the manufacturer make these promises? *You'll be a winner of first prizes—see boy's clothing. You'll be like an octopus—able to hold on tight and move your board quickly in any direction. You'll be able to speed away quickly. Using the board will make you happy—see boy's smiling face. Guide students to see that everything in the ad is designed to make the product desirable.*

- Are these claims reasonable? Do they make sense? Which claims are facts and which claims are opinions? *Skateboarding requires skills, balance and agility. These characteristics cannot be bought, but must be learned through practice. Some people have more talent at physical activities than other people; therefore, it is unreasonable for the manufacturer to claim that his skateboard can do all these things. They don't make sense. Boxes 1 and 2 on the activity sheet should contain facts, Box 4 contains opinions.*

- Why does the manufacturer put these things in their advertising? *Elicit the idea that it helps sell more skateboards, which keeps the skateboard manufacturer in business. The advertising appeals to our desire to be successful. It offers unrealistic promises that cannot be fulfilled by the product; however, it feeds someone's dreams.*

- Are there any issues about skateboards that are ignored or not addressed by the advertisement? *Health and safety issues are not addressed. Many people are concerned about the number of serious accidents involving children and skateboards.*

The boy pictured in the advertisement is not wearing a helmet or kneepads, so if he falls he could be injured more easily. Students can add this information to Box 4 in the form of questions: "Are these skateboards safe? Have people had accidents using this product?" Students might also question whether anyone has actually broken a world record with this product.

- Why do you think the manufacturer did not include safety issues in the ad? *It would probably discourage people from buying the new skateboard. The manufacturer is biased. His point of view is one-sided, or slanted, in order to convince people to buy his product.*

■ Independent Practice

Form collaborative groups of 3–5 students. Explain that each group will take a real advertisement and analyze it to determine what kind of bias they can find in the ad. They should look at the advertisement with the same critical vision they used on the Octopus Skateboard. After they work together to analyze the ad, the group will make a poster that "reveals" the truth in the advertising and separates the facts from the opinions. Show an overhead of the Real Scoop (see page 63) to help students understand how to make their posters. Provide pre-selected ads or magazines to students so that they can choose their own ads. Plan time for each group to present their poster and the real advertisement to the whole class.

■ Homework

Have students complete the Is That Really So? worksheet (see page 64) as homework. For more advanced students, assign the following questions:

1. Do you think bias can exist on the Internet? Why or Why not?

2. Where would you be most likely to find bias on the Internet?

3. Encourage all students to bring in ads that they believe are biased.

Applying Your Knowledge in Evaluating the Web

This lesson will teach students how to apply concepts from Lesson 2 while using the Internet to complete actual research activities.

NET Standards Covered: 1b, 2b, 3, 4, 5 and 6

Objectives: Students will be able to:

- apply the concept of bias to evaluate Web sites for accuracy

- locate and explore Web sites that offer opposing viewpoints about controversial situations

- identify controversial situations in their own community and research the issues involved in these situations, presenting all sides of the issue to the class

■ The Candy Bar Controversy

Materials:

- Jeremiah and the Candy Bar Controversy script (see page 65)

- large candy bar

Time: 1 class period

Directions:

1. Pick one student to play the part of Jeremiah, and ask him to take a seat at the front of the class. Jeremiah should hold the candy bar in his lap. Pick two more students to play Miss Fit and Candyman, aspects of his conscience. Give them copies of the script, and encourage them to be very persuasive in talking to Jeremiah. If possible, have the three chosen students practice their parts away from the rest of the class, so that they will feel comfortable performing in front of the class.

2. Perform the skit.

3. Ask students to remember all the reasons Miss Fit and Candyman raised as they tried to influence Jeremiah. Record all of the answers on the chalkboard. Students should recall:

   - Candy causes cavities.

   - Candy ruins your appetite.

   - Candy gives you energy.

- The energy "high" is followed by an energy "low."

- Candy is sold in grocery stores, so it must be good for you. (If students don't recognize the false logic of this statement, remind them of the counter-argument.)

- Eating milk chocolate helps dairy farmers, so you are being patriotic when you eat it. (How much milk goes into a milk chocolate bar and an individual's personal definition of patriotism are addressed here.)

- His mother told him not to do it. (An issue of personal values.)

4. Ask students to identify points that could be researched easily on the Internet. They should conclude that the first four points and part of the sixth point rely on facts that could be found on the Internet, while the issues of patriotism and personal values are not factual.

5. As a class, brainstorm the types of Web sites that could provide accurate information about the statements Miss Fit and Candyman made. Students might suggest:

   - a dental association or dentist's personal Web site

   - sites dealing with sugar

   - sites dealing with how to be healthy

   - sites about physical fitness

   - candy manufacturer's sites

   - sites giving statistics about the ingredients in milk chocolate

   - government sites, such as the Food and Drug Administration

   - non-profit consumer organizations

   - news magazines that report on public health issues

6. Share the candy bar with the class as a treat for a job well done.

■ Situations Activity

Materials:

- Situations for Practice Research worksheet for each pair of students (see page 66–67)

- 3 pieces of chart paper titled "Candy Bars," "Fur Coats" and "Pesticides"

- markers

- access to Internet

Time: 2 or more class sessions for research

Directions:

1. Inform students that they will be given some more situations to consider, and that they will work with a partner to investigate all sides of the issues at the computer lab.

2. Divide students into groups of two or three, depending on the computer resources available.

3. Pass out the worksheets so that each group has one set. Have volunteers read each situation aloud, and check for understanding of the text. Tell students that they will be doing real research on the questions raised in the situations. Emphasize that they will need to research both sides of each situation and record the URLs (Web site addresses) of the sites they visit, as well as any pertinent information they find at the Web site. Remind students how to use a search engine, and how to log on to the Internet.

4. Allow the students to begin their research on the three situations provided in this lesson. On returning to the classroom, have students record the Web sites they visited in the appropriate PRO or CON column on the chart paper for each situation. Discuss the findings as a class.

■ Research Organizer Activity

Materials:

- local newspapers
- Research Organizer worksheet (see page 68)
- Note-taking Overheads #1 and #2 (see pages 69–70)
- 3" x 5" index cards
- access to Internet

Time: 1 class session

Directions:

1. Have students use existing knowledge of local newspapers to identify several controversial issues in the community. For instance, are some people protesting new development in town? Is there a problem with pollution? Are citizens concerned about rising prices for water, sewers or trash pick-up? Does a new library need to be built? Brainstorm places where information about the issue might be found. Likely sources could be your local newspaper's Web site, your city or county government Web site, the Web site of involved developers, the local Friends of the Library club or local environmental groups.

2. Set up research groups based on student interests. Try to have each group work on a different topic so that final presentations will be varied and informative.

3. Give each group a copy of the Research Organizer and ask the group to determine which member will be the official recorder. The recorder's responsibility will be to turn in the completed Research Organizer at the end of the project. Give each group member the responsibility of preparing note cards from one of the sources they find on the Internet.

Hint: Prepare transparencies from the Note-taking Overheads if your class needs practice in learning how to take notes and use them for a mini-lesson before you begin.

Assessment:

Students will plan a group presentation that

- identifies the issue studied
- analyzes arguments in favor of and against the issue
- cites Web sources for both sides of the argument
- makes a final recommendation on how the issue should be resolved

Students should be encouraged to present their findings in a way that allows for creativity and includes all members of their group. Suggestions are: write their own drama, prepare a poster or mural, prepare a news broadcast or "interview" show or write to a newspaper about the issue.

Students may also be interested in writing a letter to the editor of the local paper or speaking at a public meeting if they develop strong ideas about their issue.

Key Concepts in Chapter 6

- Information that is true, but that does not tell the whole story, can be misleading.

- Pictures can also be misleading.

- Facts are true; opinions are just one point of view. Be aware that sometimes people state their opinions as if they were facts.

- An author who discusses only one point of view is showing bias; you should do further research to find other opinions.

"The Real Truth About Humpty Dumpty"

We go now to the Crown Court to hear the case of the Dumpty family vs. Knight McDougall.

Judge: *(Adjusts his wig and hits desk with gavel a few times.)* This court is now in session. It will now hear the opening statement of the prosecution.

Prosecution: Your Honor, I will prove that Humpty Dumpty's fall was no accident. It is clear that one of the king's men pushed him, and I will prove to you today that that man was ... Mr. McDougall. *(He points to defendant.)*

Judge: The Court will now hear the statement of the defense.

Defense: Your honor, there is absolutely no evidence for this accusation. My client Mr. McDougall asserts that he never laid a hand on Mr. Dumpty and was several feet from him when the unfortunate accident occurred. Mr. McDougall's horse Benedict was there at the time of the fall, and will verify this fact.

Judge: Prosecution, you may examine your first witness.

Prosecution: I call Horse Benedict to the stand.

Judge: Do you promise to tell the whole truth and nothing but the truth?

Horse Benedict: I do.

Prosecution: Had there been any harsh words between Mr. Dumpty and Mr. McDougall prior to this so-called "accident"?

Benedict: Well, all the king's men teased Mr. Dumpty at times, and our egg friend occasionally got a bit fried.

Prosecution: I see. In your own words, what happened on the morning of March 15?

Benedict: I was standing near the wall about to talk with Humpty when all of a sudden I heard a great, well, thud, and, oh my, what a mess. I looked over the wall, and that poor egg was toast.

Prosecution: I see, and was Mr. McDougall anywhere near Mr. Dumpty when this accident occurred?

Benedict: He was at least three or four feet away.

Prosecution: I see. Would you describe yourself as loyal, Mr. Benedict?

Benedict: Oh, yes, Sir. The most loyal. I would never be a traitor to Mr. McDougall.

Prosecution: Would you lie for him or perhaps scramble your story a bit about Egg Humpty?

Benedict: Neigh. I repeat. He did not push Mr. Dumpty.

Stop at this point and ask the class if there is any evidence regarding whether McDougall is innocent or guilty.

Prosecution: How do you feel about eggs, Benedict?

Benedict: I've always been quite fond of most eggs. Especially with Hollandaise sauce. Oh, you mean like Humpty. Well, he was a bit of a push-over, I mean, er, I don't think he was all he was cracked up to be, oh dear, but ...

Prosecution: And did you push Mr. Dumpty?

Benedict: I never laid a hoof on him, Sir. Not one.

Prosecution: Did you lay anything else on him? The truth, Benedict, the whole truth!

Benedict: *(Pause.)* Well, I may have sort have shall we say, nudged him a bit, but ... but ... he made me do it. *(Pointing to McDougall.)* I had gone up to talk with Dumpty and just as I raised my head, McDougall kicked me with his spurs and, well, it didn't take much. McDougall never liked Humpty. He said Dumpty had been in the sun too long and was a rotten egg.

Prosecution: I rest my case.

• • • • • • • • • • • • • • • • • • •

The End

Consider the Source

Media Analysis

For Sale

The _____

_____

only $ _____

1

Look at What You Get

-
-
-
-

2

Pie in the Sky Promises

-
-
-
-

3

?

4

Instructions

1. Identify product and price.
2. Record special features of product.
3. List stated or implied promises.
4. Identify issues that the ad ignores or minimizes.

The Real Scoop on The Octopus

Conclusion: This octopus is hiding behind an ink cloud! Buyer beware!

Evaluation Criteria for Web Sites: Bias

Name: _____   Date: _____

Is That Really So?

Decide whether each statement is a FACT or an OPINION, then circle the letter in the appropriate column. Match your answers with the numbered spaces at the bottom of the page to answer the title question.

	Fact	Opinion	Statement
1.	M	A	Computers have many uses.
2.	C	S	Everyone needs a computer.
3.	R	M	Computers always give accurate information.
4.	T	D	The World Wide Web is like an electronic library.
5.	P	E	The World Wide Web should be controlled.
6.	Y	F	E-mail is a very fast way to communicate.
7.	W	S	Junk email is annoying.
8.	O	L	Yahoo and Google are search engines.
9.	G	I	AOL is the best Internet Service Provider.
10.	E	H	WWW stands for the World Wide Web.
11.	S	U	Dot-gov is the major domain label for government Web sites.
12.	B	E	The Internet gives you the best information available.
13.	L	N	Children should be allowed to use computers every day.
14.	O	K	Some families do not own computers.

Is that really so?

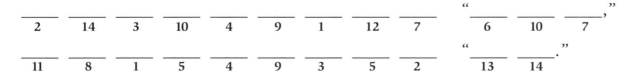

$\overline{}$ $\overline{}$ $\overline{}$ $\overline{}$ $\overline{}$ $\overline{}$ $\overline{}$ $\overline{}$ $\overline{}$ " $\overline{}$ $\overline{}$ $\overline{}$,"
2 14 3 10 4 9 1 12 7   6 10 7

$\overline{}$ $\overline{}$ $\overline{}$ $\overline{}$ $\overline{}$ $\overline{}$ $\overline{}$ $\overline{}$ $\overline{}$ " $\overline{}$ $\overline{}$."
11 8 1 5 4 9 3 5 2   13 14

Jeremiah and the Candy Bar Controversy

Characters: Jeremiah, Miss Fit, Candyman

Setting: Jeremiah sits on a chair, holding a large candy bar in his lap. Miss Fit and Candyman, his consciences, stand at his left and right shoulders.

• • • • • • • • • • • • • • • • • • • •

Jeremiah begins to pick up the candy bar, but just as he starts to unwrap it—

Miss Fit: Don't do it, Jeremiah! You know your mom said she didn't want you to eat any candy right before dinner.

Candyman: Hey, she'll never know. She doesn't even know you bought this candy bar with your allowance.

Miss Fit: Jeremiah, you'll know you disobeyed, besides, you don't want to get any more cavities, do you? What did the dentist say?

Candyman: Oh, forget the dentist. You can brush your teeth later. And it will taste sooooo good.

Miss Fit: *(Sarcastic.)* Well, it might taste good now—but how will you explain not being able to eat any of your favorite dinner? Remember, Mom's making spaghetti.

Candyman: Aren't you feeling a little tired? This chocolate will boost your energy and you'll get your homework done faster!

Miss Fit: Oh yeah? You'll get a sugar high, and then you'll get a sugar low, low, low! Don't do it!

Candyman: Don't listen to her! Sugar is good for you. If it wasn't, why would they sell it in the grocery stores? After all, that's the same place they sell vegetables!

Miss Fit: So what? That's the same place they sell dishwashing detergent and motor oil, too. You wouldn't put those in your tummy, would you?

Candyman: Hey, it's not only going to taste good, it's part of your patriotic duty! If you don't eat that milk chocolate bar, some poor dairy farmer isn't going to make enough money to feed his family. You'd better do it.

Both Consciences: *(Together, look at the audience and say …)* What do you think? Let's research the good and bad effects of eating sugar.

• • • • • • • • • • • • • • • • • • • •

The End

    Evaluation Criteria for Web Sites: Bias **65**

Situations for Practice Research

Record the information you find as instructed in each situation.

1. What's for Lunch?

Bill is thinking about having a large ice cream sundae for lunch, but decides first to go onto the Web to get the scoop on the health values of sugar. He finds an article at Kandybars.com. Should he stop there or continue to look for other articles? If he does more research, which types of sites should he check out? (Circle as many as apply.)

a. a health organization site   **b.** a sugar cane grower's site   **c.** an ice cream company's site

If you circled all three, you're right! Finding accurate information usually requires that we use more than one source. Now you're ready to visit the Internet and see what you can find out. Type the words "effects of sugar" into your favorite search engine. The search engine will provide you with a list of sites that contain information about your topic.

Look at the results and notice that the URL for each site is listed at the END of its description. Find an article that looks interesting from a dot-com (.com), as well as a dot-org (.org), dot-edu (.edu) or dot-gov (.gov). Try to find two articles that your classmates will understand, and print them out to bring back to class. Record the URL of each Web site here:

• URL #1: _____   • URL #2: _____

2. Help, I'm freezing!

Larissa lives in Minnesota where winters are very cold. She grew three inches last summer and needs to buy a new winter coat. At the mall she saw a rabbit skin parka that was beautiful and warm. It was on sale, so she was tempted to buy it, but she had mixed feelings about buying something made of real fur. A friend of hers convinced her to get some facts and to read some opinions on the Internet before making a decision.

Help Larissa by going to a search engine (such as Google) and typing in "fur coats." You will likely find many sites listed, including sites sponsored by coat makers and sellers, sites sponsored by animal rights groups (against fur coats) and sites belonging to individuals who express their personal opinions on the subject. Find and read at least one article in favor of fur coats and one against them. Write the Web site addresses in the spaces provided, then list some pros and cons.

Web site in favor of fur coats:

_____

Pros:

Web site against fur coats:

_____

Cons:

Situations for Practice Research (continued)

Will Larissa buy the fur coat? We'll never know because it's a personal decision, but at least she will be able to make an informed choice.

If you were Larissa's friend, what would your advice be? _____

_____

_____

3. The Case of the Missing Tomatoes

Kevin's neighbor Mrs. Frost is growing tomatoes this year. Last summer insects destroyed her tomatoes. She is thinking about using pesticides this year or growing them in a planter inside her house where they would have better protection. She asked her friends what they think about the dangers of pesticides, but they all had different opinions. Kevin has offered to help her do some research on the Internet so that she understands all of her choices.

Kevin and Mrs. Frost go to a search engine and type in the words "pesticide dangers" on the search line. There they find many articles to choose from, including several that describe dangers of pesticides, a few that express a belief that environmentalists are overly concerned about the use of pesticides and some government sites (such as the Food and Drug Administration) that present research facts.

If you were Kevin, how would you go about helping Mrs. Frost find out about the effects of pesticides? What words could you type in the search line that might lead her to find solutions that she can be sure are non-toxic?

Outline your research plan below, then use it to find information on at least three different sites to make a recommendation to Mrs. Frost.

Research Plan:

_____

_____

_____

_____

URLs of Web Sites Visited: **Sponsor of Site:**

1. _____   _____

2. _____   _____

3. _____   _____

Record the information you find at each site and your recommendation to Mrs. Frost.

Research Organizer

Group Members: _____

Our Issue: _____

Why is this issue controversial? _____

Our Plan (Where will we look for information?) _____

	URL	Date Visited	Title of Article	Author of Article or Name of Sponsoring Organization	Article Point of View: PRO or CON
1.					
2.					
3.					
4.					
5.					

Print copies of the articles and attach them to this worksheet.

Read each article and summarize its major points. Be sure to find articles that discuss both sides of your issue. Record your findings on another sheet of paper or on index cards so that you can prepare your group presentation for the class.

Note-taking Overhead #1

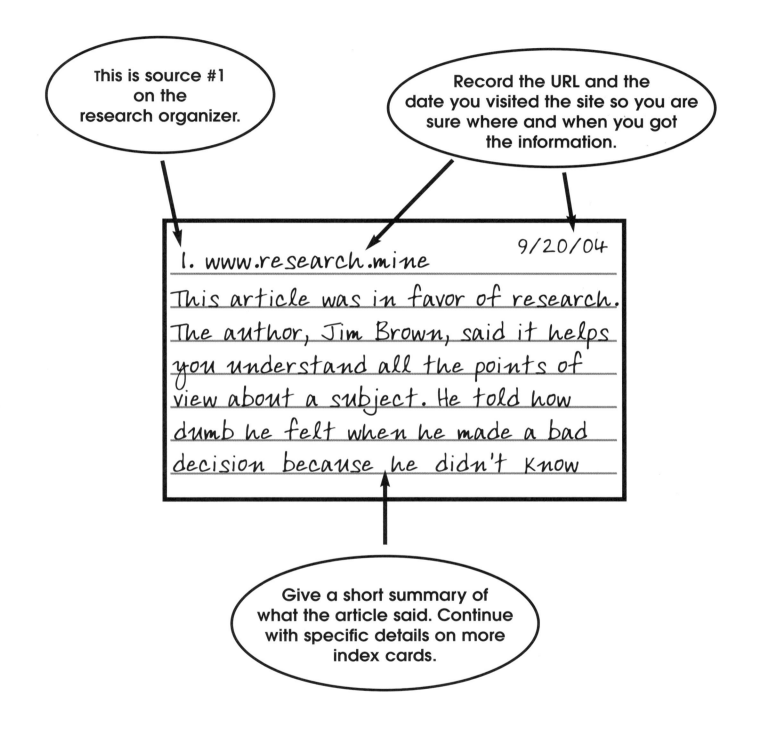

This is source #1 on the research organizer.

Record the URL and the date you visited the site so you are sure where and when you got the information.

9/20/04

1. www.research.mine

This article was in favor of research. The author, Jim Brown, said it helps you understand all the points of view about a subject. He told how dumb he felt when he made a bad decision because he didn't know

Give a short summary of what the article said. Continue with specific details on more index cards.

Evaluation Criteria for Web Sites: Bias

Note-taking Overhead #2

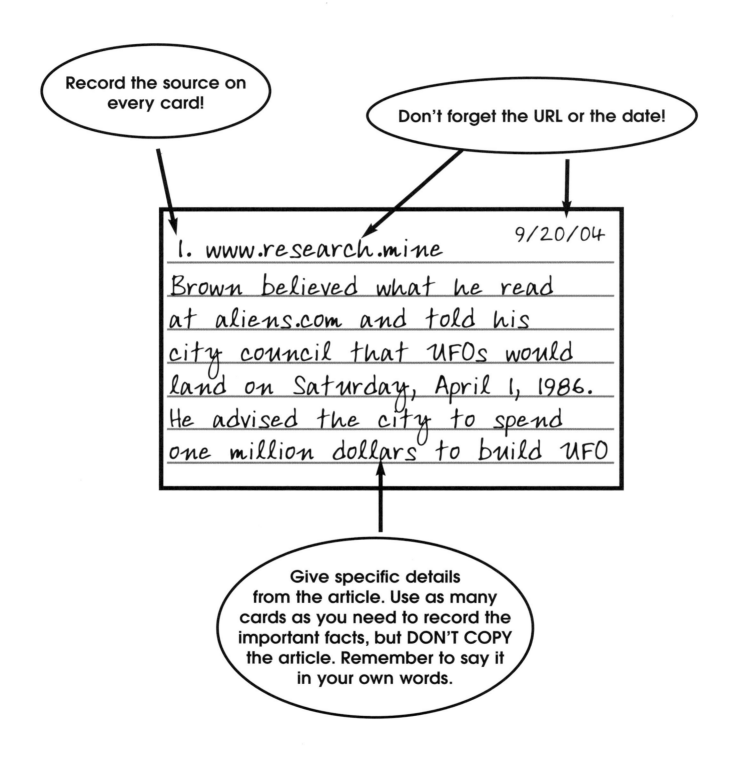

Record the source on every card!

Don't forget the URL or the date!

9/20/04

1. www.research.mine

Brown believed what he read at aliens.com and told his city council that UFOs would land on Saturday, April 1, 1986. He advised the city to spend one million dollars to build UFO

Give specific details from the article. Use as many cards as you need to record the important facts, but DON'T COPY the article. Remember to say it in your own words.

Evaluation Criteria for Hoaxes, Scams and Paranormal Phenomena

This chapter will help students learn to recognize hoaxes and scams, which are very common on the Internet. It will also introduce students to spoofs so that they can enjoy them without being taken in or confusing them with factual information. Drama is used in this chapter as a teaching tool to maximize student engagement.

Terms Introduced

- authentic
- chain letter
- deception
- forgery
- hoax
- legitimate
- netlore
- scam
- spoof
- urban legend

Lesson Plan 1

What are Hoaxes?

NET Standard Covered: 2a, 2c

Objectives: Students will be able to:

- identify hoaxes and classify by general type
- compare similarities and differences in famous hoaxes
- generalize and develop a set of rules to help identify hoaxes from examples used in class

■ Hoaxes Activity

Materials:

- Why People Play Hoaxes worksheet for each student (see page 76)

- Hoaxes Note-taking Sheet (see page 77)
- chart paper to record key points of discussion for reference throughout the unit

Time: 45 minutes

Directions:

1. Ask students to think of a time they were fooled or tricked and write a short paragraph about the event, including how they felt when they found out the truth. (Alternatively, they may write about a time they fooled someone else.) Have them include the reason they thought they had been tricked, or why they tried to fool another person (i.e., Was the trickster trying to be funny? What was the trickster's motive?) Have partners share their writing with each other, then ask for several volunteers to read their paragraphs to the class.

2. Tell students they will be learning about some times when many people were fooled and that these kinds of tricks are usually called "hoaxes," a word that means deception.

3. Pass out the worksheet and note-taking sheet. Have students read the activity sheet with a partner and fill in the note-taking sheet together.

4. Use the following questions to guide a classroom discussion: Why do you think e-mail is the most popular part of the Internet for spreading hoaxes? Why do people forward this type of mail to their friends? What would happen if someone took a hoax into a chat room?

5. Record key points on chart paper to display and refer to throughout this unit.

Optional: Have students make a bulletin board featuring the key points for extra credit.

Lesson Plan 2

Identifying Hoaxes

NET Standard Covered: 2a, 2c

Objectives: Students will be able to:

- identify key clues found in most Internet hoaxes

- evaluate information to determine whether it is likely a hoax

■ Saving Who? Activity

Materials:

- "Saving Who?" script (see pages 78–80)

- Key Clues written on sentence strips (see top of pages 81–82)

- Famous Hoaxes and Real Situation Cards, 1 set per group (see pages 83–84)

- sheets of red and green paper, 1 each per student (The paper will not be written on, so it will be reusable. Half sheets will work as well.)

Time: 45 minutes

Prepare in Advance:

Make audience cue cards for the script. They should read:

- And now, here they come!

- Who? Who? Who?

- Urgent, Urgent, Urgent!

- Help! Help!

- Tell everyone! Tell everyone!

- Hurry up! Hurry up! Do it right now!

- Where? Where? Where?

- He's going to die if we don't help. Oh, no! Oh, no! Oh, no!

Write the key clues from the top of page 81 on separate sheets of paper so they are in sentence strips.

Directions:

1. Ask a student to look up the word "melodrama" and share the definition with the class. Emphasize that the emotions in this type of drama are intended to be exaggerated.

2. Choose five students to act out the parts of the melodrama. Give them time to practice their lines. While they practice, explain to the rest of the class that during a melodrama, the audience also has an important part to play. Their lines will be cued by the "director."

3. Have the cast perform the melodrama. The director should indicate when it is time for the audience to participate.

4. Following the skit, pass the key clues sentence strips out to four students. Ask them to stand and read the key clue to the class, then post it on the wall. Have students analyze the skit and write down which part corresponds to each key clue.

5. Pass out the Situation Cards and Key Clues worksheet. Explain that each group has received cards that describe hoaxes and real situations. Their job is to decide if the situation described on the card is a hoax or something real. They should use the Key Clues to help make their decisions, and be ready to defend their decisions to the class.

6. Give the groups time to work together.

7. Ask for volunteers to read the Situation Cards aloud. Have the groups hold up red sheets of paper if they think the situation is a hoax and therefore shouldn't be forwarded, and green sheets if they think the information is legitimate. Discuss their decisions, reinforcing the idea that every hoax does not contain all four of the key clues. The key clues, however, do help frame the kinds of questions critical thinkers should keep in mind as they evaluate any request for action. Additionally, many hoaxsters are try-

> Beware! All kinds of tricks can be played with cameras and photography software, including morphing objects and adding items to pictures that don't belong. So if you see a picture of a UFO on the White House lawn, think twice.

ing to make money, so often there is an appeal for a "donation" included in a hoax.

8. Reveal which situations were real and which were hoaxes. Add that even well-informed adults often have problems telling the difference between real situations and hoaxes. Hoaxes have become a major problem on the Internet because they waste a lot of time (and sometimes money) and often cause a lot of needless concern. Because they are such a widespread problem, there are special Web sites that track and expose hoaxes. A few of them are:

- www.hoaxbusters.org

- www.snopes.org

- www.nonprofit.Internet/hoax

- www.museumofhoaxes.com

Remind students that if they ever wonder whether something on the Internet is real or a hoax, they should **always** ask a knowledgeable adult, such as a parent, teacher or librarian.

Can you think of any movies or TV shows you have seen that included hoaxes as part of their stories? A few possible answers would be: TV shows—*Scooby Doo, Candid Camera;* movies—*Quiz Show, Catch Me If You Can.*

Additional Activity:

With guidance from a responsible adult, go to the hoax reference sites described above and find an example from each of these categories: virus, give-away, chain letter, sympathy plea and hacked history.

Lesson Plan 3

Is This for Real?

NET Standards Covered: 2a and 2c

Objectives: Students will be able to:

- define "spoof" and related words

- become aware that certain Web sites and e-mails are intended to be spoofs and may be only partially factual or not at all true

- learn cues that tip off Internet readers that information is meant as a spoof

■ Skit Activities

Materials:

- Skit 1 from page 85—piece of paper, pig and wolf masks *(optional)*

- Skit 2 from page 86—costumes and 2 lanterns *(optional)*

Time: 45 minutes

Prepare in Advance:

1. Choose one or both of the skits for your class. Skit 2 works best for students who have studied the American Revolutionary War.

2. For Skit 1: No preparation needed.

3. For Skit 2: Review Henry Wadsworth Longfellow's "Paul Revere's Ride" and discuss the historical background of the poem.

Directions:

1. Perform one or both skits with your class.

Urban Legends

We all know that the difference between a fact and a rumor is that a fact is true, while a rumor may be true, false or only partly true. Until facts are known, you can't be sure how true rumors are because they can get started in odd ways and can become very distorted as they spread.

There are many stories circulating on the Internet. Some are started deliberately as hoaxes, while others may simply be built on top of rumors by people who didn't bother to get their facts straight or who were attempting to get attention. If a story is widely circulated on the Internet, it is often referred to as an urban legend or urban myth. Like a rumor, it may be true, false or somewhere in between. This type of netlore usually describes something bad happening to a person or animal, and asks the reader to take some kind of action. It generally sounds believable, even though there is no real evidence.

Keep in mind that since many, if not most, urban legends are untrue, it is important to check out a story's authenticity with one of the hoax reference sites before passing it on to someone else.

2. Explain that the skits are spoofs and ask students what they think a spoof is. Students should understand that a spoof is a joke or a take-off on something else. Indicate that other words for spoof are: parody, mockery, satire, take-off and farce. Write the words on the board.

3. Discuss what is being mocked in the spoof.

4. What if we weren't familiar with "The Three Little Pigs" or if we didn't know the historical background of "Paul Revere's Ride?" Would the spoof be funny? Students should realize that for a spoof to be understood, the audience needs to be in on the joke or understand the original situation that is being mocked.

5. Pair off students or have them form small groups and write down the names of any TV shows, radio shows or movies that are spoofs or that regularly feature spoofs. Some answers might include: *Mad Magazine,* the Naked Gun series (movies), *The Daily News* (TV show), *Saturday Night Live* and *Goldmember.* Write down all reasonable answers. If you are not familiar with an answer, ask the student to explain what the spoof is mocking. Get a consensus from the rest of the students as to whether it qualifies as a spoof.

6. Discuss what possible hints we use to tell us it is meant to be a spoof and not a real situation. Answers might include: funny costumes, funny voices, exaggerated statements, body language and gestures. These are auditory and visual cues.

7. Ask students: "If you are reading a spoof on the Internet, do you have the advantage of auditory and visual cues?" Guide them to realize that it is hard to recognize a spoof especially if there are no pictures or sound included with the site.

■ Additional Activity

Ask students to write a spoof, either individually or in small groups, to present to the class in the form of a skit or written play. They can spoof a person or any form of media. A fairy tale makes a fun and not too difficult target for a spoof. (If they choose to spoof a person, suggest that people at the school are off-limits.)

Paranormal Phenomena

Paranormal topics such as fortune telling, ESP and UFO's may be featured on Web sites or in various other areas on the Internet. Since students occasionally ask to do reports on them or come across them on the Internet, it may be useful to share the following:

- sometimes sites about paranormal phenomena are placed on the Internet as hoaxes, money-making scams or attention-getters

- some information is placed there by sincere individuals who believe they have special abilities (such as ESP) and/or who have done careful research

It is important to differentiate between the above types of information. Students may want to compare material they find on the Internet with information from library books (generally found in the DDC 030 section of nonfiction), which has been edited and carefully screened.

Key Concepts in Chapter 7

Hoaxes are:

- found in e-mail more than any other area of the Internet

- started by people who like to fool other people and/or who are trying to make money off gullible Internet users

Be suspicious of an e-mail if it:

- says a situation is urgent

- says some type of action is needed right away

- uses real sounding names of people or places, but gives no information as to how to verify their legitimacy

If in doubt, check a hoax Web site such as:

www.hoaxbusters.org

www.snopes.org

www.nonprofit.Internet/hoax

www.museumofhoaxes.com

If still in doubt, don't forward the e-mail to your friends. The majority of e-mails with the above characteristics are hoaxes.

Remember these facts about spoofs and paranormal phenomena:

- A spoof is a take-off or mockery of a person or situation.

- Unlike a hoax, the purpose of a spoof is not to fool readers (Internet users), but rather to include them in on the joke.

- To understand the spoof, the reader needs to be familiar with the person or situation being mocked. If not, he or she may think that the information is real.

- Some examples of paranormal phenomena on the Internet are fortune telling, ESP and UFO's.

Why People Play Hoaxes

In 1835 an American newspaper, *The New York Sun,* reported life on the moon. All sorts of things had been seen, it said, from bison-like animals to man-bats. Reporters said their information came from the *Edinburgh Journal of Science* in Scotland and was based on findings supplied by a highly regarded astronomer named John Herschel, who had seen life on the moon through his powerful telescope. None of it was true, of course, but the newspaper got away with it until one of the reporters admitted to a friend that it was all made up. So much for life on the moon.

In 1946 a struggling artist named Elmyr de Hory found that he could paint in the styles of famous artists like Pablo Picasso and Henri Matisse and then pass off his own work as their originals. For 20 years he got away with it until a curator tried to clean one of the paintings. The paint had not yet totally dried and came off with the dirt. Once the public had the "dirt" on Mr. de Hory, he ended up in prison.

Challenge: Today *The New York Times* obviously could not get away with claiming life on the moon because we know so much about the moon now. But occasionally journalists do get caught falsifying information to get the public's attention or make themselves look good. Go to a search engine and type "journalists AND hoaxes." See if you can unearth any modern day journalistic hoaxes as well as some other interesting ones from the past. Share them with your class.

Often a "hoaxer" wants to see how far he or she can go in fooling others, but sometimes he or she has another motive too, such as trying to make money, as in the case of the art forger de Hory. Hoaxes involving money-making schemes are often referred to as scams. Even *The New York Sun's* hoax was somewhat motivated by money, as the publishers correctly thought that their sales would go up after they starting running the intriguing stories about life on the moon.

What makes hoaxes believable? Hoaxers make the situation sound authentic by naming real places and people or sometimes places or people that just sound real. In the case of *The New York Sun,* the writers reported their articles were based on information from the *Edinburgh Journal of Science.* Although the journal had actually existed at one time, it was no longer in business, but few people in this country knew that. Also, they quoted the scientist John Herschel, who was also real, but who was doing research in Africa and didn't even know he was being quoted as part of the hoax.

In the case of the art forgeries, Mr. de Hory studied the artists he copied and was very knowledgeable about their styles, so he was very convincing when he sold the paintings.

Many hoaxes will go further; they will try to scare their victims. When people are frightened, they often do not reason well and will fall for just about anything.

Hoaxes Note-taking Sheet

Read "Why People Play Hoaxes" with a partner. As you read, see if you can find the answers to these questions.

1. **Describe what the hoaxes have in common.**

    _____

    _____

    _____

    _____

    _____

2. **Name two reasons people play hoaxes.**

    a) _____

    b) _____

3. **What's another name for a hoax that involves making money off of other people?**

    _____

4. **What do you think usually happens to people who are caught "pulling off" a scam?**

    _____

5. **What Internet system is most used for spreading hoaxes?**

    _____

Unscramble these letters to read a famous quote:

A LOFO DNA SHI YNOEM REA ONOS ADTPER.

___ ____ ___ ____ ___ ____

____ _____ _____.

"Saving Who?"

Characters: Narrator #1; Narrator #2; Sarah, a teenager who just got her first computer; Maria, Sarah's best friend; Danny, a boy in Sarah's class; Trevor, Danny's best friend

Setting: In the lunch area at Compuville Junior High School.

• • • • • • • • • • • • • • • • • • • •

Narrator #1:   *(Talking to Narrator #2 and gesturing at the audience.)* Wow, look how many people made it back for today's episode of Life at Compuville High! *(Looking at the audience, speaking enthusiastically.)* Hey, guys! Welcome back! If you'll remember, yesterday was Sarah's birthday and at the end of the show she was just going home to her family birthday party. Let's listen in and see how it turned out.

Narrator #2:   But before we drop in on Sarah and her friends, don't forget that whenever _____ *(insert Narrator #1's real name here)* or I hold up one of these "cue cards," everyone has to read the words aloud.

Narrator #1:   Let's practice! *(Hold up cue card that says: **And now, HERE THEY COME!**)*

(Sarah and Maria walk on stage.)

Maria: So Sarah, I'm dying to know … what was in that **huge** box your Mom was hiding in the closet for your birthday?

Sarah: You'll never believe it!! I just about died!! It was my very own computer!

Maria: WOW! Now we can send each other e-mail!

Sarah: I know—and my dad already got it hooked up and I'm online now. I even got my first e-mail, **last night**, just a few minutes after my dad plugged in the computer!

Maria: You did??? Who was it from?

Narrator #2:   *(Hold up cue card: **WHO? WHO? WHO?**)*

Sarah: *(Don't speak until audience is quiet again.)* It was from Beverly, and it was serious.

Maria: Beverly?? Beverly Who?

Narrator #2:   *(Hold up cue card: **WHO? WHO? WHO?**)*

Sarah: I don't know, just Beverly—anyway, that is not what's important. What's important is what she told me. It's really, really, really important—and urgent, too!!

Narrator #1:   (Hold up cue card: **URGENT, URGENT, URGENT!**)

Maria: Well, tell me then—what's so urgent from Beverly Somebody?

(Danny and Trevor walk in.)

Danny: Hi, Maria. Hi, Sarah. Did I hear someone say something was urgent?

Sarah: Oh, hi Danny, hi Trevor. Yes, I got an urgent message from Beverly last night on my new computer. I'm glad you're here—the more people that hear about this the better. There's a boy in the hospital and he's going to die if we don't do something about it!

Narrator #2:   (Hold up cue card: **HELP! HELP!**)

Trevor: That does sound urgent, but what can we do? We're only kids.

Maria: Why is he going to die? Is it anyone we know?

Danny: Yeah, what happened?

Sarah: Well, Beverly says that he almost got run over by a car and now he's in the hospital, but his mom can't pay for the operation.

Trevor: That sounds bad. What kind of operation does he need?

Sarah: I'm not sure, but the most important thing is that she asked me to tell all of my friends about it. And, she said the hospital will do the operation for free if we get 200 people to send them an e-mail!

Maria: How is just sending e-mail going to pay for an operation? That doesn't make sense.

Sarah: *(Annoyed)* How should I know? It's what Beverly said.

Narrator #1:   (Hold up cue card: **TELL EVERYONE! TELL EVERYONE!**)

Danny: Great! Send it to me and I'll forward it to everyone on my list.

Trevor: Gosh, Danny, you're right—I can send an e-mail to everyone on my soccer team—and I'll ask them to tell their friends, too! Let's go!

(Danny and Trevor start to leave.)

Narrator #2:   (Hold up cue card: **HURRY UP! HURRY UP! Do it right now!**)

(Trevor suddenly runs back to the girls.)

Trevor: Wait a minute, Sarah—what hospital should they write to?

Sarah: Beverly didn't say—but there's only one hospital in Compuville, so send it there.

Evaluation Criteria for Hoaxes ...

Narrator #1: (Hold up Cue Card: **WHERE? WHERE? WHERE?**)

(Trevor turns around and leaves.)

Maria: Well, Sarah, it looks like Danny and Trevor are going to help you spread the word, but I still wonder who this Beverly person is. And did she tell you who got hit by the car? And if it's so urgent, why didn't she tell you the boy's name and what hospital he's in?

Sarah: *(In a disgusted tone of voice.)* Oh Maria, what's wrong with you? Sometimes you ask so many questions. Don't you care about this poor kid? This is a matter of life and death!! We can't investigate every little detail. I'll see you later—I'm going to go home and forward Beverly's letter to some more people. *(Sarah leaves.)*

Narrator #2: *(Hold up cue card:* **He's going to die if we don't help. Oh, no! Oh, No! Oh, No!***)*

Maria: *(Thinking out loud.)* Hmmm, I never heard of anyone named Beverly …

Narrator #2: *(Hold up cue card:* **WHO? WHO? WHO?***)*

Narrator #1: Well, folks, thanks for joining us for today's episode of Life at Compuville Junior High. It looks like Sarah got the present she was hoping for, and now she's going to save the world! Tune in tomorrow for the next installment.

● ● ● ● ● ● ● ● ● ● ● ● ● ● ● ● ● ● ●
The End

Key Clues

Key Clues help you tell the difference between a **real appeal** for help and a **hoax**, or false appeal. Analyze the situation cards your teacher gives you by answering these four questions about each situation. Then decide: Is this a hoax? Or is it a real appeal for help?

Key Clues:

1. Does the message claim that the matter is urgent?

2. Does the message ask you to forward it to all of your friends right away?

3. Does the message threaten that something bad, or unlucky, will happen to you if you don't follow its instructions?

4. Does the message tell you where it came from? Do you know the person who originally wrote the message, or is it just being passed on by someone you know? Can you verify its truth?

Write your answer to each question in the boxes.

Situation #1	My Decision
1. _____ 2. _____ 3. _____ 4. _____	☐ Real ☐ Hoax

Situation #2	My Decision
1. _____ 2. _____ 3. _____ 4. _____	☐ Real ☐ Hoax

Situation #3	My Decision
1. _____ 2. _____ 3. _____ 4. _____	☐ Real ☐ Hoax

Key Clues (continued)

Situation #4	My Decision
1. _____ 2. _____ 3. _____ 4. _____	❑ Real ❑ Hoax

Situation #5	My Decision
1. _____ 2. _____ 3. _____ 4. _____	❑ Real ❑ Hoax

Situation #6	My Decision
1. _____ 2. _____ 3. _____ 4. _____	❑ Real ❑ Hoax

Situation #7	My Decision
1. _____ 2. _____ 3. _____ 4. _____	❑ Real ❑ Hoax

Situation #8	My Decision
1. _____ 2. _____ 3. _____ 4. _____	❑ Real ❑ Hoax

Famous Hoaxes Situation Cards

Situation #1:

Several magazines have reported that millions of wild duck eggs are being collected and shipped to New York City. The eggs are a source of dried albumen, which is used in photography, candy-making and leather manufacturing. Send money **now** to stop this theft and protect wild ducks or North America's duck population will face extinction. Make sure all of your friends and acquaintances are informed of this problem.

Situation #2:

The new Compuville Zoo is asking citizens to contribute to a building fund for a new lion exhibit. They hope to build a larger, more natural environment so their three lions do not have to live in the small cages they currently occupy. Any individual or group who wants to help in this important project can contact Ms. Hope Fullness at 555-1314.

Situation #3:

This week a farmer in north Idaho announced an important discovery. It seems that the mysterious bones he uncovered while plowing his potato field are the remains of a previously unknown species of dinosaur. Although the University has asked to have the bones donated to their museum, the farmer claims they are his property and he will resist every effort to have them taken away. He is, however, letting the public view his discovery for the mere cost of $10. The sheriff is threatening to take the bones into protective custody—so if you want to see them, you'd better hurry!

Situation #4:

The local blood bank is making an **urgent** plea with all citizens who have type O blood to come in to donate blood. Compuville Hospital is extremely low on this blood type and fears that lives may be lost if the reserves are not increased. If you can help the blood bank by donating blood, please call 555-5454 and make an appointment with Lois Needleman, R.N., the blood bank director. You can also drop into their headquarters at 2121 East Rose Avenue. All donors receive free cookies and juice, plus the satisfaction of knowing they have helped their fellow citizens.

Famous Hoax Situation Cards (continued)

Situation #5:

Are you worried about pollution? Do you want to do something about it? If so, join the members of the Compuville Environmental Society and take part in some of their urgent, ongoing projects. This week they are leading a hike into the Appleton Mountains to clean up the most popular hiking trail. Dues are only $25 a year. The next meeting will be Monday at 7 P.M. at the Hale Branch Library on East Street.

Situation #6:

NWPS, the National Waterfowl Protection Society, claims that water pollution is killing 10 million swans every year in their Arctic breeding grounds. If you want to help protect these beautiful birds, you must act now. The best way to help them is to send a $10 donation to Arnie Honker, the president of the society. He reports his address is General Delivery, Gainesville, AK. Please hurry!

Situation #7:

The following article was published in *The Compuville Chronicle* on April 1, 1996. "The White House announced today that it will be selling one of our nation's most beloved monuments. The Lincoln Memorial, in Washington, D.C., has become so expensive to maintain, that the White House has agreed to sell it to the Ford Motor Company. Although the sales price has not been announced, it is expected to be millions of dollars. All money raised will be used to reduce the national debt. The Ford Motor Company is expected to rename the monument. It will be known as the Lincoln-Mercury Memorial from now on. The exact date of the sale has not been announced."

Situation #8:

Andrew Burns, a student at Newton Elementary School, needs your help. He was recently diagnosed with cancer and his father is out of work. With hospital bills increasing every day, his poor mother is in urgent need of money. Compuville Clinic has set up a trust fund for his medical expenses. The Newton Parent Association has pledged to donate money from their pizza fundraiser this Saturday at Tony's Pizzeria. Come on down and eat some pizza to help Andrew, or send a donation directly to the Compuville Clinic, 800 E. Healthy Blvd. All donations are tax deductible and receipts will be mailed.

"The Three Little Pigs Revisited"

Narrator: As you all know, the third little pig, the smart little pig, built his house out of bricks. Last we saw of the wolf, he was at the pig's door disguised in a lamb's costume. That attempt failing, he's found a new approach. We go now to the home of the third little pig, where all three pigs are safe behind their locked front door.

Wolf: *(Raps on door twice.)* Knock, knock.

Pig 1: *(Looks through the peep hole.)* Who's there?

Wolf: City Building Inspector.

Pig 2: City Building Inspector who?

Wolf: *(Paws on hips.)* This isn't a knock-knock joke. Open up.

Pig 3: No way! What do you want?

Wolf: I have to knock your house down. *(He points to a wrecking crane.)*

Pig 1: What do you mean you have to knock our house down?

Wolf: I have a paper here. See? It says right here—this part of the forrest isn't zoned for brick buildings.

Pig 2: Wait a minute! "Forest" is spelled wrong. Why, that's a phony paper.

Wolf: Oh, no! I should have used the spell checker! *(He opens his mouth wide and growls.)*

Pig 3: Oh, my, but what big teeth you have!

Wolf: The better to eat you with!

Pig 1: Hey, Wolf, you're in the wrong story. Scram!

Wolf: You started it! Say, can you give me directions to Grandma's house?

● ● ● ● ● ● ● ● ● ● ● ● ● ● ● ● ● ● ●

The End

"The Lights are Out in the Belfry"

Have three students perform this skit, which spoofs Paul Revere's friend as he gets ready to hang the lanterns in the Old North Church.

Narrator:	As you may know, on April 18, 1775, the American patriot Paul Revere set up a plan to warn colonists in the Boston area of an attack from the British Red Coats. A friend was go to the belfry tower of the Old North Church and send a signal to Revere, who was waiting on the other side of the River. The signal would let him know how the Red Coats were approaching. The friend was to hang one lantern if the British were coming by land, and two lanterns if they were coming by sea. Revere and two others would then ride around the area to warn the colonists. Come with me now, as we see Revere and his friend re-enacting this fateful night.
Friend:	Okay, Revere, let me see if I've got this right. I hang one lantern if the Red Coats are attacking by land and two if they are getting into their boats to go by sea. Right?
Revere:	That's it. Now for heavens sakes, don't mess this up. Remember the time . . .
Friend:	No, no, now never mind about that. I've got this down. *(Revere gallops off.)*
Friend:	One if by land and two if by sea, one if by land and two if by sea. Perhaps I should write that down. Oh dear, no quill or bottle of ink with me. Well, that's easy enough. I can certainly keep that in my head.
Friend:	*(Revere's friend starts walking around, cupping his hand to his ear, listening for the British.)* My but it's awfully quiet tonight. No sign of the Red Coats yet. Guess I'll just sit down here for a spell and count the stars in the sky. One, two, three, four, five, six, seven, ... ten, thirty, forty, *(snore)* ...
Narrator:	*(Holds up a card that says "20 minutes later." Begins pounding a constant rhythm on a drum or flat surface, first quietly, then a little louder.)*
Friend:	Oh, my gosh. I must have fallen asleep. Blimey, there they are, the Red Coats. I can hear them in the distance. *(Narrator pounds louder.)* Now I see them. They're getting into their boats. That means. . . they're attacking by sea! To the tower! *(He pretends to be climbing stairs.)* Now what was it, one lantern if they were coming by land and two if they were coming by sea, or was it, one if by sea, and two if by land? Oh, dear. *(He sighs and starts pacing, then stops and pulls a coin out of his pocket.)* What the heck—heads, one lantern; tails, two. *(He flips the coin. Then smiles and holds up two lanterns. He shrugs.)* "I mean, how important can this be? In a week no one will even remember what happened tonight.

Chat Rooms and E-mail

The majority of schools do not permit students to access personal e-mail accounts or visit chat rooms. Viruses and "worms" are spread rapidly through e-mail, undesirable information cannot be filtered out and most of the information passed through these venues does not support the academic curriculum. On the other hand, students do use these forums at home and need to be instructed in proper etiquette and safety when using these areas of the Internet. They also need to be aware of their own responsibility in not creating and/or spreading misinformation. In addition, this chapter provides activities that highlight the advantages and disadvantages of using chat rooms and e-mail for research.

Terms Introduced

- auditory cues
- flame
- visual cues

Lesson Plan 1

Chat Rooms

NET Standard Covered: 4

Objectives: Students will be able to recognize that while chat rooms are generally not good places to find authoritative information, they can be used to obtain a variety of opinions, get good leads on subjects that can be explored further through reputable sources and check out rumors or debunk hoaxes (covered in more detail in Chapter 7).

■ Chat Room Activity

Materials:

- Chat Room True or False worksheet (see page 91)
- Verifying Chat Rooms (see page 92)

Time: 45 minutes

Directions:

1. Hand out the Chat Room True or False worksheet. When all of the students have completed it, go over the answers, indicating that only number 4 is false. Follow up with a discussion as to why Internet users can't be sure of what they read in chat rooms.

2. Ask the class which types of Internet communication they think are most carefully written—chat rooms, Web sites or e-mail. Which are the least carefully written?

3. Students should arrive at the conclusion that generally Web sites are the most carefully written and chat rooms are the least. In chat rooms, people are typing fast to keep up with conversation and don't always think their thoughts through before they type. However, when it comes to doing research, think of chat rooms as you would brainstorming. You may get suggestions that aren't very valuable, but if you get even one or two that are, the chat room may have been worth your time.

4. Copy the following examples for students to read and answer individually or in small groups. Guide students to realize that in Example 1, although James had to "wade" through some information that he couldn't use, he was able to get some valuable suggestions. In Example 2, if Lynn was looking for opinions, she went to the right place. If she was looking for facts, she was better off looking elsewhere.

Example 1: James is doing a science project on the Doppler Effect. With his parents' guidance, he goes into a chat room to see if anyone can explain exactly what the Doppler is. Unfortunately there is no one in the particular chat room he chooses who can give him a very accurate explanation. However, someone directs him to www.fi.edu. He goes to that Web site and gets the information he needs. In addition, someone else gives him another suggestion about demonstrating the Doppler Effect by recording a siren as it approaches and vanishes, and using recording as part of his science exhibit. Was it worth his time going to the chat room? What did he get out of it?

Example 2: Lynn went to a chat room to get information about issues in a coming election. What do you think she is most likely to get, facts or opinions?

5. Pass out the Verifying Chat Rooms worksheet. Form small groups and direct students to brainstorm which reliable sources could be used to verify the claims.

6. Ask a student volunteer to look up the word "accountable." Discuss why accountability is not present in chat rooms, guiding students to realize that there is no way to hold chatters responsible for what they say, and sometimes they will say just about anything.

Lesson Plan 2

E-mail

Students in elementary school use e-mail to keep in touch with their friends (even if their friends live just next door). They are also beginning to use it to obtain information for research projects. This lesson will focus on issues of effective e-mail communication and netiquette, without which wrong information is often conveyed.

NET Standard Covered: 4

Objectives: Students will be able to:

- learn about netiquette
- learn about abbreviations that clarify communication

■ E-mail Activity

Materials:

- Darlene's E-mail (see page 93)

Time: 30 minutes

Directions:

1. Talk with students about clues they have for knowing if someone they are talking to is being serious, funny or sarcastic. Write all reasonable answers on the board that relate to tone of voice, gestures and body language and facial expressions.

2. Explain that these are all auditory and visual cues that clarify the meaning of a person's words through signals we can hear and see.

3. Give each student a copy of Darlene's E-mail. Have students read the first letter silently. Then ask if they think the writer is being serious or sarcastic, instructing them to give "thumbs up" if they think Darlene is having a great time on her visit, and "thumbs down" if they think she can't wait to come home.

4. Ask for a volunteer to read it in a way that makes it sound as if Darlene is having a really good time, and another volunteer to read it in a way that she is not. Have the students note that only the reader's tone, inflection and facial expressions give us the auditory and visual cues we need to understand how Darlene is feeling.

5. Now ask the students to "punctuate" or embellish the story, choosing Internet abbreviations or emoticons from the word bank and placing their selections at the end of each sentence, per the directions. For a more complete list of abbreviations, they can visit penpals.englishclub.com/abbreviations.htm.

6. Ask students if they know where to find "emoticons" on the Internet. If no one responds, suggest that typing the word "emoticons" under keyword options in an e-mail system will lead them to a broad selection.

■ Rules of Netiquette Activity

Materials:

- NetiQuiz (see page 94)
- index cards

Directions:

1. Write the word "etiquette" on the board and ask students what it means, guiding them to the idea that it refers to proper manners. Have them illustrate by naming some rules of etiquette to be used at a dinner table.

2. Break students into small groups for the NetiQuiz. Inform them that some of the information comes from the chapter but some of it is based on common sense.

3. Ask questions aloud one at a time. Each group will be asked to come up with one answer only, then write their answer (A, B or C) on a card. When you ask for a show of cards, a representative from each group will hold up the group's card. If he or she gets the right answer, the team gets a point. The group with the most points at the end wins. If all of the teams get all of the questions correct, give a reward, such as extra free time in class.

Note: Prior to giving the test, review the term flame, meaning an angry (or insulting) e-mail or chat room posting.

"I Don't Remember Asking for This ..."

Spam is unsolicited (unrequested) e-mail that is usually sent by companies trying to sell their products and services. It is sent out as bulk e-mail, usually to thousands of people at once, and often times Internet users receive 30 or more in a day.

People who send the spam buy lists of e-mail addresses from companies that use robotic (automatic) software to get e-mail addresses from various places on the Internet. When you receive spam, you have not been personally selected to get it. It might seem like it because your name may even appear in the title of the e-mail, but you are just one of thousands of people whose e-mail was automatically located by this special software and whose name was automatically inserted. Just like junk mail sent to your home through the mail, spam can sometimes look very important. It can say **urgent** or **important** to get your attention, so beware!

Key Concepts in Chapter 8

- Be sure to get your parents' permission before going into a chat room.

- You will "meet" all different kinds of people in chat rooms. Some are knowledgeable; others are not. Don't believe everything you read.

- Although information you read in chat rooms is not always reliable, chat rooms can be very valuable for finding:
  - a variety of opinions
  - good leads that you can verify through trustworthy sources such as books, reliable Web sites and experts in your community

- It is extremely important to follow the rules of good "netiquette." Not only is it respectful to others, but it results in more effective communication and fewer misunderstandings.

Name: _____ Date: _____

Chat Room True or False

For each of the statements below, place a "T" or an "F" on the line to indicate if you think the statement is true or false.

In a chat room of strangers, the types of "chatters" you may meet include:

1. _____ People who are very intelligent, and are very careful about telling the truth.

2. _____ People who are very intelligent, but sometimes mistaken.

3. _____ People who are not very well-informed, but think they are, and who will say almost anything to impress others.

4. _____ People you know you can trust 100%.

5. _____ People who have a distorted view of reality.

6. _____ People who will lie about themselves.

7. _____ People who are very kind and helpful.

8. _____ People who are very hateful and say mean things.

9. _____ People who pretend to be nice but who are not.

10. _____ People who have bad intentions.

11. _____ People who mean well, but who give bad advice.

Name: _____   Date: _____

Verifying Chat Rooms

Some chat rooms are specialized. For example, they may be geared for certain groups such as writers, bungee jumpers, historians, card players or stamp collectors. In some of these groups there may be experts present who can verify the information discussed. However, you may wish to ask about the expert's background to see what his or her qualifications are or if he or she is likely to have any particular type of bias.

Statement: Verify Statement	What type of books, Web sites or experts would you use to find out if the statement is true or false?
"I hear that we are expecting a tornado tomorrow."	
"Sea turtles may be extinct in 25 years."	
"Molasses cures arthritis."	
"The composer J. S. Bach had 40 children."	
"Chocolate isn't good for dogs."	
"More people were killed in the Civil War than any other American war."	
"Kids who suck their thumbs will need braces later."	

Darlene's E-mail

Read this e-mail. Can you tell if the writer is being serious or sarcastic?

Hi, Anna. Sorry I haven't written for the past few days. I went to visit my aunt and uncle on their farm and they don't have a computer. I had a really great time. I got up every morning with my uncle at five to milk the cows. In the afternoon I baled hay and made biscuits. My aunt and uncle's TV was broken, so in the evening we sat in their living room and talked about what life was like on the farm when they were growing up. It was so much fun I hated to come home.

Your best friend,
Darlene

Add Internet abbreviations in the spaces below to make it clear that the writer truly was having a good time at her aunt and uncle's.

Hi, Anna. Sorry I haven't written for the past few days. I went to visit my aunt and uncle on their farm and they don't have a computer. I had a really great time. _____ I got up every morning with my uncle at five to milk the cows and in the afternoon I baled hay and made biscuits. _____ My aunt and uncle's TV was broken, so in the evening we sat in their living room and talked about what life was like on the farm when they were growing up. It was so much fun I hated to come home. _____

Your best friend,
Darlene

Add Internet abbreviations in the spaces below to make it clear that the writer was NOT having a good time, but was being sarcastic.

Hi, Anna. Sorry I haven't written for the past few days. I went to visit my aunt and uncle on their farm and they don't have a computer. I had a really great time. _____ I got up every morning with my uncle at five to milk the cows and in the afternoon I baled hay and made biscuits. _____ My aunt and uncle's TV was broken, so in the evening we sat in their living room and talked about what life was like on the farm when they were growing up. It was so much fun I hated to come home. _____

Your best friend,
Darlene

Abbreviations:

LOL (laugh out loud)   **JK** (just kidding)   **TIC** (tongue in cheek)   **LTIP** (laugh till I puke)

:) (smile)   ;-) (wink)   :-((frown)

Name: _____   Date: _____

NetiQuiz

1. **If you are in a chat room, it is a good idea to:**

    a. treat both friends and strangers with respect

    b. say whatever you'd like—you really can't hurt anyone's feelings

    c. be insulting, if you'd like; no one knows who you are and can't figure it out

2. **In a chat room, if people say something you know is incorrect:**

    a. Tell them they're stupid. They have no right to say something unless they have checked it out first.

    b. Correct them politely and tell them where you got your information.

    c. Don't say anything. Who cares what you think?

3. **In a chat room or e-mail, if someone "throws flames" at you:**

    a. get their names and addresses

    b. throw flames back at them

    c. tell them you're not looking for an insult match and if necessary, discontinue the conversation

4. **E-mail that you don't request and get from people you don't know is called:**

    a. scam

    b. spam

    c. netijunk

5. **In a chat room,**

    a. jump right into the conversation as soon as you enter the chat room; otherwise you're likely to lose your nerve

    b. follow the conversation for a moment or two so that you understand the background of what's being said

    c. try to control the conversation, otherwise you may not get enough turns to say what you want

6. **In a chat room or e-mail, it is not a good idea to type in all capitals because the people you are corresponding with will think you are:**

    a. lazy

    b. angry

    c. ignorant

Consider the Source

Applications

This chapter provides a wealth of ideas for projects that upper elementary students can accomplish using Internet resources. Because young students are just beginning to develop analytical skills that allow them to evaluate the credibility of Internet sources, we recommend that students be encouraged to use multiple types of sources in all research projects. Plagiarism has proliferated due to the ease of copying and pasting Internet articles into research documents, therefore, it is also important to instruct students on what plagiarism is, why it is wrong and how to avoid it. An additional safeguard against plagiarism is requiring a bibliography in all research projects.

This chapter begins with a lesson on developing and using effective key word searches. Research challenges follow for the core academic areas: language arts, social studies, science and math. Links to sites that will help students be successful Web researchers are included. Each research suggestion engages students in all of the National Education Technology Standards, so individual standards are not cited in each challenge.

Lesson Plan

Effective Key Word Searches

As students begin to conduct their own research on the Internet, they need to discover how to formulate effective key word searching skills. There are no right or wrong answers in how to go about searching. In general, however, an effective search will result in a manageable number of Web sites to visit, and those Web sites will contain information directly related to the subject being researched.

This lesson offers students a hands-on opportunity to use the kid-friendly Yahooligans.com to research information for imaginary research paper topics. The first two activities include several key word phrases to search for and ask students to record the number of hits they find for each one. They should conclude that both too much and too little information in the search phrase gives ineffective results. The second half of the assignment asks students to brainstorm several alternative key word searches, and then try them on the computer. Finally, they are asked to use metacognitive skills to describe the thinking process they used while creating their own key word searches. A natural follow-up to these activities are the individual research challenges.

NET Standards Covered: all

Objectives: Students will be able to:

- investigate and compare the results of using different key word search terms for the same topic

- record data about the search results

- draw conclusions about the kind of key word searches which are most effective

- create their own key word searches and investigate the results of varying the search terms

- analyze the metacognitive process they used in forming the search terms

■ Key Word Activity

Materials:

- Key Word Searching worksheet (see pages 99–100)

- pencils

Time: 45 minutes

Prepare in Advance: Because of the rapidly changing nature of the Web, we recommend that you complete the worksheet a day or two before students go to the lab in order to have accurate numbers for questions 1 and 2, and to have the opportunity to think about your own metacognitive process as you develop key word search phrases for questions 3 and 4.

Directions:

1. Read and discuss the introductory information at the top of the worksheet before you begin. Have the students complete the online portion of the worksheet independently, giving help when needed. The most common error students make is misspelling words or typing incorrectly. If students come up with no hits for any of the entries, inspect their spelling first.

2. At the end of the computer work time, gather students together and record the answers they found for questions 1 and 2. The numbers of Web sites counted should be the same for all students since they are using the same search engine and the same key word phrases. They should conclude that letters "e" and "d" gave the best information for questions 1 and 2 respectively.

3. A common student misconception is that finding more sites is better. This is only true if the sites are directly related to the research they are doing. In question 1, choice "d" gives the most hits, but many of them are related to desert tortoises or tortoises in other parts of the world. These Web sites would not be useful for a report limited to Galapagos Island Giant Tortoises. On the other hand, inputting "Galapagos Island tortoises" results in fewer sites, but each site contains information that is directly related to the subject of the report. Likewise, in question 2, choice "c" results in over 20 sites related to mummies, but most of them pertain to ancient Egypt. Qualifying the key word "mummies" with the descriptor "Incan" results in sites that only have information about ancient Incan mummies.

4. Questions 3 and 4 ask students to develop their own key word phrases. Have the students work in small groups, sharing the phrases they created, as well as the results they obtained. Each group can report phrases that produced helpful information and

phrases that were not productive. Record both types on the board or overhead to find commonalities in each group.

5. Reinforce the idea that there are no set rules in how to find information, and that locating good sources is often a matter of redefining search terms based on prior results. This is also a good time to reinforce the role of the librarian as a reference helper. When students are doing independent research, instead of becoming frustrated over too few or too many results, they should consult a reference librarian, teacher or other adult for help in defining their search terms.

Tip: Teach students the trick of putting quotation marks around key words that they always want to find together. For instance, "macintosh apples" will mainly return articles about a type of fruit, while Macintosh apples will return articles about apples, raincoats, the MacIntosh clan and Macintosh computers! Even the addition of quotation marks will not eliminate every reference to unintentional topics, but a recent search for "macintosh apples" at Yahoo reduced the number of Web site hits to 1,320 from 40,400 for the same key words.

Challenges

■ Language Arts Challenge: Biography of an Author

Researching the life of a contemporary author gives children the opportunity to investigate fact and opinion. Learning to tell the difference between facts and opinions is a key skill that must be used when evaluating source information of all kinds. It is especially critical when using web-based information due to the speed with which information can be published and changed.

Challenge Outline:

This project asks students to use Internet resources to investigate and document the life of a favorite author. Students should search for facts about the author, such as birth date, childhood, education and published works. They can also locate opinion-based information from online interviews with their subject and reviews of their writings.

Students can present their information as a traditional written report or as a Power Point presentation. Technology-based presentations are a wonderful way to showcase your students' work at open houses or during parent conferences—and they don't require lots of storage space!

Suggested Resources:

- Judy Blume, author of the Fudge books and many others, has her own Web site, www.judyblume.com, that offers students both biographical facts, a publishing history and her opinions on the issue of book censorship. It includes photos of Ms. Blume and links to many other sites.

- Gary Paulsen's site is managed by his publisher, Random House, at www.randomhouse.com/features/garypaulsen. It contains an abundance of biographical information, a letter from Gary to his readers, lists of his awards and information about many of his books.

- J. K. Rowling, author of the Harry Potter series, can be found at www.scholastic.com/harrypotter. Although Rowling is a very private person, many interviews with her have been published, and transcripts can be found on the Web.

- Jon Scieszka, author of *The True Story of the 3 Little Pigs* as well as other fractured fairy tales, is found at www.baloneyhenryp.com. This site includes pictures, short biographies, links to information about his books, games to play, screensavers to download and even information on the latest book signing tour.

An advantage of this challenge is the ease with which novice researchers can find information. Students can use any search engine and simply type the author's name into the search window. They will feel successful right away!

■ Math/Science/Social Studies Challenge: Biographies of Famous People

Adapting Challenge 1 for use in math, science or social studies is as simple as choosing a famous person instead of an author. Names of famous scientists, politicians, athletes, inventors, business people, philosophers and philanthropists are readily available on the Internet or in your library's biography section.

Challenge Outline:

Have students use a key word search starting with the words "list of _____ (famous scientists, famous mathematicians, famous kings and queens, famous politicians, etc.)" on any search engine. Multiple sites containing the names of people who have influenced the formation of world civilizations will be identified. Students might appreciate www.blupete.com/Literature?Biographies/Science/Scients.htm because it includes a one-paragraph summary of each scientist.

In lieu of including published works and reviews of their subject's writings, students can make a timeline of the famous person's life, a summary of how their discoveries or actions impacted the world and how their discoveries were received by the society in which they lived.

As with Challenge 1, key word searching is very easy because students only have to type the person's name into the search engine.

■ Science/Social Studies Challenge: Recent History

This challenge encompasses anything of importance that has occurred in the last 40 years.

Challenge Outline:

Students pick a controversial topic of interest, such as the civil rights movement, a presidential election, cigarette use and abuse, homework, space exploration, global warming, protection of archaeological sites, habitat destruction, endangered animals, etc. Their research should include: facts about the subject, opinions about what should have been done about the issue and the outcome of the issue, if one exists.

Students present their research in written, oral or Power Point form. Their reports should show that they clearly understand the difference between the facts they uncovered and the opinions people held at the time. Once again, separating the facts from the opinions will help students identify statements that are particularly likely to contain misleading or inaccurate information. Have the students use the Research Log on page 101 for recording facts and opinions.

■ Math/Science Challenge: Ancient Discoveries, Modern Inventions

Scientists and inventors have changed history by uncovering the rules of Euclidean geometry; inventing the airplane, telephone and computer; discovering penicillin and the smallpox vaccine; and splitting the atom.

Challenge Outline:

Have students pick an invention or discovery that changed civilization. They should research the discovery and record all the ways that life changed because of it. Then create a triangular prism display (see page 102 for a how-to) that shows a before and after "snapshot" of the world. Include a written description of how the discovery was made.

To help students realize that misinformation can even exist in fact-heavy research, ask them to check whether more than one person claimed to invent or discover their topic. How will they decide whom to believe?

Be sure to include a bibliography on the display board.

■ Social Studies/Geography/Earth Science Challenge: The Earth as Others Have Seen It

This challenge is a good collaborative group project, and it is wonderful to display at open houses or during parent conference week. A successful project requires students to use many higher level thinking skills as they analyze, compare and evaluate the information they find at different Web sites.

Challenge Outline:

Have the students investigate the history of maps. Use the Web to find maps of the world made in ancient times, the middle ages and the sixteenth through twentieth centuries. How have they changed? What accounts for these changes? Use a "science fair" display board to showcase maps that have been downloaded from the Internet in chronological order. Paragraphs describing each map and noting the differences from prior maps can be included as captions.

Have students use the planning worksheet on pages 103–104 to record information for four maps. Make extra copies if the students should compare more than four maps.

Key Word Searching

How can you find the information you want in a library that is as big as the whole world? The answer is: Use a search engine! Just as a real engine needs fuel to run, a search engine needs its own "gas." **Key words** are the fuel you put into the search engine. Getting useful results from the search engine depends on using the *best* key words. Many helpful Web sites can be overlooked if you use too many key words. Using words that are too specific can also limit the number of sites that are found. On the other hand, if the words you choose are too general, you might be directed to hundreds of Web sites and locating the ones that have information you can use would take too long and be frustrating.

Go to www.yahoo.com and click on the word "kids" in the "fun" category on the left-hand side of the page. You will be taken to the Yahooligans home page where you will find a search window near the center of the page. Now you're ready to start.

The following are the names of some reports that might be written for school. Under the title of the report you will find a list of key word searches that could be used to find information for the report. Type each one into the search window, then click on the "search" button. Count how many Web sites are found and record the number on the line next to the key word.

1. **Feeding Habits of Galapagos Island Giant Tortoises**

    a. feeding habits of Galapagos Island tortoises _____

    b. tortoise food _____

    c. Galapagos Islands _____

    d. tortoises _____

    e. Galapagos Island tortoises _____

    Which key words gave the best information for your report?

    _____

2. **Mummification Practices of the Ancient Incas in Peru**

    a. mummification practices of the ancient Incas _____

    b. mummification in Peru _____

    c. mummies _____

    d. Incan mummies _____

    Which key words gave the best information for your report?

    _____

Key Word Searching (continued)

Here are titles for two more reports. List the key words that you think will help find accurate, detailed information to help you write the report. Then type them into the search engine and see what happens.

3. **From Maize to Corn on the Cob, an Agricultural History of a Modern American Food**

    a. _____

    b. _____

    c. _____

    d. _____

Which key words gave the best information for your report?

_____

4. **Castles and Cathedrals: How Europeans Constructed Buildings without Modern Machinery**

    a. _____

    b. _____

    c. _____

    d. _____

Which key words gave the best information for your report?

_____

Think about it!

Describe the thinking strategies you used to pick the key words you tried. Share your strategies with your class. It's important to talk about the ones that worked best and the ones that didn't.

_____

_____

_____

_____

_____

_____

Name: _____   Date: _____

Research Log

Use this research log to record the facts and opinions you gather in your research. Use a new log for each different Web site.

Topic: _____

URL: _____   **Date Used:** _____

Facts	Opinions

Triangular Prism Display

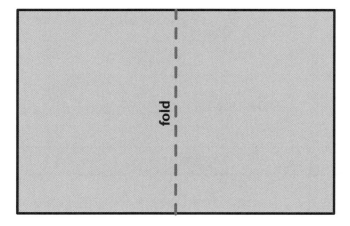

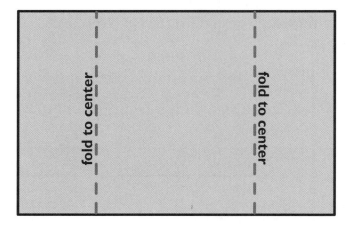

Step 1

Use two pieces of 12" x 18" construction paper. Fold one in half, as pictured above.

Step 2

Fold the second piece so that the ends meet in the middle, as shown above.

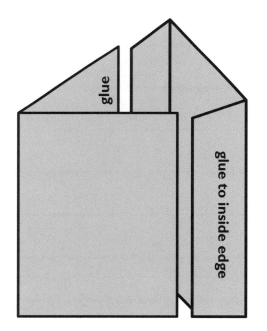

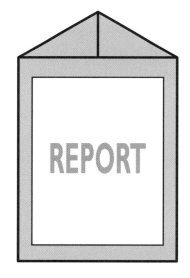

Step 3

Glue the short ends of the second piece to the inside of the first piece of construction paper, forming a triangular display.

Step 4

Mount the finished report on the three sides of the display.

Name: _____ Date: _____

Planning Sheet for
The Earth as Others Have Seen It

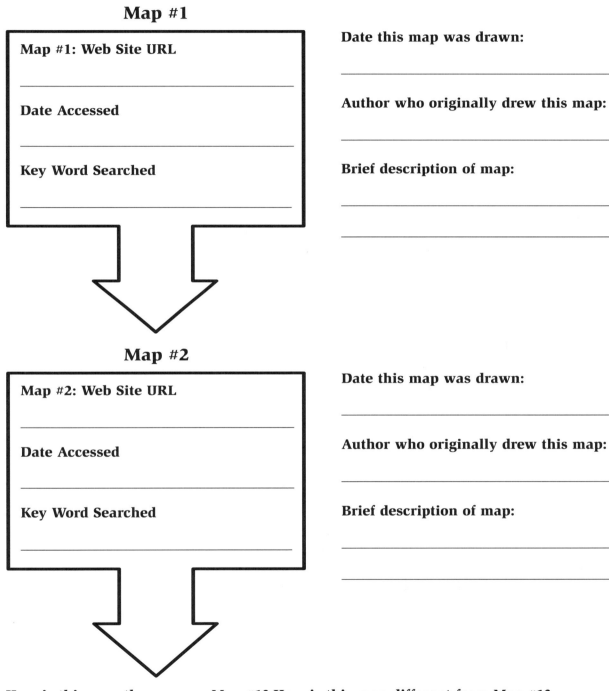

Map #1

Map #1: Web Site URL

_____

Date Accessed

_____

Key Word Searched

_____

Date this map was drawn:

_____

Author who originally drew this map:

_____

Brief description of map:

_____

_____

Map #2

Map #2: Web Site URL

_____

Date Accessed

_____

Key Word Searched

_____

Date this map was drawn:

_____

Author who originally drew this map:

_____

Brief description of map:

_____

_____

How is this map the same as Map #1? How is this map different from Map #1?

_____

_____

Planning Sheet (continued)

Map #3

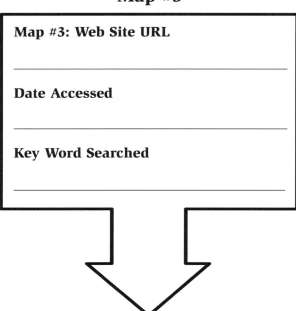

Map #3: Web Site URL

_____

Date Accessed

_____

Key Word Searched

_____

Date this map was drawn:

_____

Author who originally drew this map:

_____

Brief description of map:

_____

_____

How is this map the same as Map #2? How is this map different from Map #2?

_____

_____

Map #4

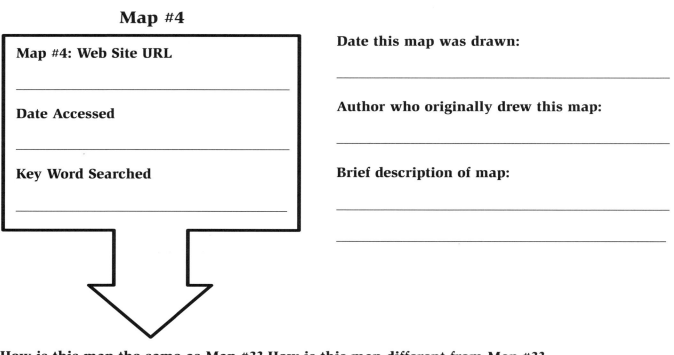

Map #4: Web Site URL

_____

Date Accessed

_____

Key Word Searched

_____

Date this map was drawn:

_____

Author who originally drew this map:

_____

Brief description of map:

_____

_____

How is this map the same as Map #3? How is this map different from Map #3?

_____

_____

10 Creative Application: Developing a Responsible Web Site

In this chapter students will design a mock Web site. Dedicate a bulletin board to post illustrations of Web pages. *Optional:* Have the class actually register its site for a fee on the Web. Resources for site development and registration are provided.

Lesson Plan

Developing a Web Site

NET Standards Covered: all

Objectives: Students will be able to:

- review parts of a Web site

- choose content for their own class (mock) Web site

- learn to responsibly maintain a site

■ Designing a Web Site Activity

Materials:

- overhead

- paper and pens

- access to the Web

- large bulletin board

Time: initial lesson plan will require 1 class period plus homework assignments

Directions:

1. Show a transparency of the Sample Home Page sheet (see page 107) and point out the following: title, which may or may not be accompanied by a logo or graphic; body copy (text), which describes the scope of the site; and framed or unframed site links, which show connections to other Web pages within the same site (internal links) or to other sites (external links).

2. Explain to the students that they are going to design a Web site pertaining to their class activities. Add that this is a mock site (unless you decide to actually put it on the Web), and that it will be featured on a class bulletin board. If an ongoing project is desired, the bulletin board will be dedicated to the project and modified periodically to reflect changes in the Web site.

3. Divide the class into small groups. Ask each group to brainstorm topics they would like to have on their Web site. Possibilities might include: an academic topic being studied and which will change every month (e.g., Columbus discovering America, Magellan's voyage, etc.); school news, such as individual or team athletic achievements; community events, such as a the coming Fire Department's Pancake Breakfast; or class team sports.

4. Take ideas from all of the groups and write them on the board. Have students vote and choose four ideas that they want to place on the class Web site. These will become their internal (inside) web links. If the Web site is an ongoing project, students will update/maintain their links periodically throughout the school year. The class can be divided into groups, with each group responsible for keeping their links up to date. External (outside) links to other Web sites may also be chosen (such as the school's or school district's Web site, the police department, the city's site or whatever might relate to the topics chosen for the class site).

Homework:

After the class has decided what internal links they will have, divide the class into small groups so that each group is responsible for developing the Web page for their assigned link. (In other words, if sports is a link, one of the groups will be responsible for designing the graphics and writing the text for that Web page link.) Allow class and homework time for completing the project.

Next Class Period:

1. After all of the Web pages have been designed and written, have students critique each other's Web pages, checking to see if the grammar and spelling are correct and if the information is current.

2. Ask each group to be responsible for choosing an external link, if possible one that relates to their assigned subject matter, making sure that they choose Web sites that are appropriate, accurate and up to date. Remind students about safety issues:

    • do not put pictures of themselves on the site

    • do not include their last names (or other traceable identifying information)

Designing the Layout:

Hold a contest for design of a logo or other graphic, such as a drawing of a mascot that will be placed on the home Web page to represent the class. The class as a whole can design the layout of the home page and write the body copy (which describes the purpose of the Web site), or these tasks can be assigned to smaller groups. Ask a student to then make a draft of the home page on a large piece of paper, which will be centered on a bulletin board. As link pages are written or updated throughout the year, they are placed around the home page, with titles that reflect link titles on the home page and arrows showing the links. A sample of a home page and corresponding bulletin board is shown on pages 107–108.

Advanced Options:

1. Instead of developing and maintaining a Web site as a whole class, divide students into smaller groups of four to five each, and have each group be responsible for maintaining a "bulletin board Web site" on topics related to current studies. One group would put theirs on the board one month, another group, the next month, etc.

2. Develop a real Web site and register it on the Web. There are several Web sites which provide instruction on development. You can locate them by typing "web site development" or "web site design" on the search line of a search engine. You can find an easy to follow site written for children at artsedge.kennedy-center.org/professional_resources/howto/web_develop.html. Also, there are books, such as The Internet for Dummies, that contain easy to follow instructions. The cost for registering a site is about $70; however, teachers are often able to obtain free or very inexpensive sites. For a list of companies that register Web sites, type in "web site registrar" on a search line. Permission from your school district may be required.

Sample Home Page

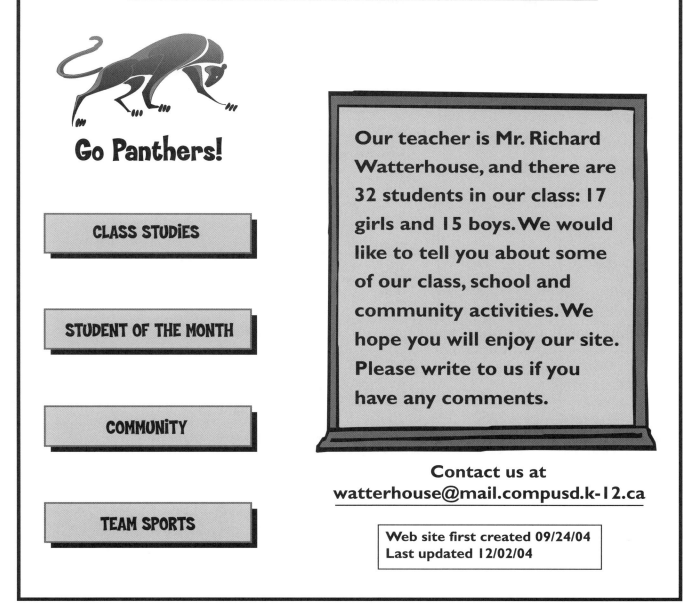

Home Page

Mr. Watterhouse's 5th Grade Class Lincoln Elementary School Compuville, USA

Go Panthers!

CLASS STUDIES

STUDENT OF THE MONTH

COMMUNITY

TEAM SPORTS

Our teacher is Mr. Richard Watterhouse, and there are 32 students in our class: 17 girls and 15 boys. We would like to tell you about some of our class, school and community activities. We hope you will enjoy our site. Please write to us if you have any comments.

Contact us at
watterhouse@mail.compusd.k-12.ca

Web site first created 09/24/04
Last updated 12/02/04

Sample Bulletin Board

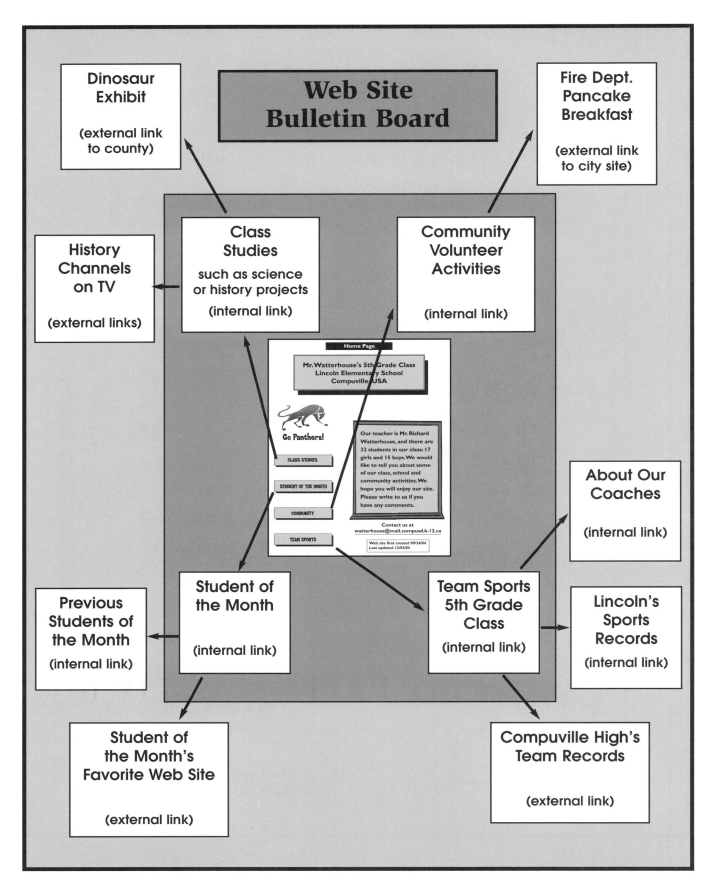

Dinosaur Exhibit

(external link to county)

Web Site Bulletin Board

Fire Dept. Pancake Breakfast

(external link to city site)

History Channels on TV

(external links)

Class Studies

such as science or history projects
(internal link)

Community Volunteer Activities

(internal link)

Home Page

Mr. Watterhouse's 5th Grade Class
Lincoln Elementary School
Compuville, USA

Go Panthers!

CLASS STUDIES

STUDENT OF THE MONTH

COMMUNITY

TEAM SPORTS

Our teacher is Mr. Richard Watterhouse, and there are 32 students in our class: 17 girls and 15 boys. We would like to tell you about some of our class, school and community activities. We hope you will enjoy our site. Please write to us if you have any comments.

Contact us at
watterhouse@mail.compusd.k-12.ca

Web site first created 09/24/04
Last updated 12/02/04

About Our Coaches

(internal link)

Previous Students of the Month

(internal link)

Student of the Month

(internal link)

Team Sports 5th Grade Class

(internal link)

Lincoln's Sports Records

(internal link)

Student of the Month's Favorite Web Site

(external link)

Compuville High's Team Records

(external link)

Scope and Sequence
National Education Technology Standards (NETS)

Appendix A

Detailed information on the National Education Technology Standards is available at www.iste.org.

Standard	Ch1 L1	Ch1 L2	Ch1 L3	Ch2 L1	Ch2 L2	Ch3 L1	Ch3 L2	Ch3 L3	Ch4	Ch5	Ch6 L1	Ch6 L2	Ch6 L3	Ch7 L1	Ch7 L2	Ch7 L3	Ch8 L1	Ch8 L2	Ch9	Ch10
NET Standard 1: Basic Operations and Concepts																				
a. Students demonstrate a sound understanding of the nature and operation of technology systems.	X	X		X	X														X	X
b. Students are proficient in the use of technology.				X									X						X	X
NET Standard 2: Social, Ethical and Human Issues																				
a. Students understand the ethical, cultural and societal issues related to technology.			X				X		X		X	X		X	X	X			X	X
b. Students practice responsible use of technology systems, information and software.		X									X	X	X						X	X
c. Students develop positive attitudes toward technology uses that support lifelong learning, collaboration, personal pursuits and productivity.	X	X		X	X				X		X	X		X	X	X			X	X
NET Standard 3: Technology Productivity Tools																				
a. Students use technology tools to enhance learning, increase productivity and promote creativity.		X										X							X	X
b. Students use productivity tools to collaborate in constructing technology-enhanced models, prepare publications and produce other creative works.	X											X							X	X

Scope and Sequence (continued)

	Ch1 L1	Ch1 L2	Ch1 L3	Ch2 L1	Ch2 L2	Ch3 L1	Ch3 L2	Ch3 L3	Ch4	Ch5	Ch6 L1	Ch6 L2	Ch6 L3	Ch7 L1	Ch7 L2	Ch7 L3	Ch8 L1	Ch8 L2	Ch9	Ch10
NET Standard 4: Technology Communications Tools																				
a. Students use telecommunications to collaborate, publish, and interact with peers, experts, and other audiences.		X				X											X	X	X	X
b. Students use a variety of media and formats to communicate information and ideas effectively to multiple audiences.		X				X							X				X	X	X	X
NET Standard 5: Technology Research Tools																				
a. Students use technology to locate, evaluate, and collect information from a variety of sources.		X				X		X	X	X			X						X	X
b. Students use technology tools to process data and report results.		X				X				X			X				X	X	X	X
c. Students evaluate and select new information resources and technological innovations based on the appropriateness for specific tasks.		X				X	X	X	X	X			X						X	X
NET Standard 6: Technology Problem-solving and Decision-making Tools																				
a. Students use technology resources for solving problems and making informed decisions						X		X	X	X			X						X	X
b. Students employ technology in the development of strategies for solving problems in the real world						X		X	X	X			X						X	X

Answers to Worksheets

Chapter 1

■ Tangled Communications (page 18)

- e-mail—a way to send messages to mailboxes over the Internet

- Internet—worldwide computer network

- World Wide Web—huge electronic library with lots of information

- chat room—place people can write back and forth in real time

■ Internet Systems (page 19)

- Find recent articles about robots in space? *World Wide Web*

- Have a group discussion about the referee's call at the ice hockey game? *chat room*

- Write to a wildlife rescue center in Australia to find out how they help injured kangaroos? *e-mail*

- Find articles about Hinduism? *World Wide Web*

- Contact a veterinarian at the Bronx Zoo to find out how dental care is provided to alligators? *e-mail*

- Discuss the president's recent speech with people around the country? *chat room*

■ The A-maze-ing Message Machine (page 20)

- What did you notice about the way each message traveled?

Each message went through at least one router.

■ Who's Watching? (page 22)

Today the Internet is used by **millions** of people all over the **world**. The inventors of the Internet didn't expect it to become such a huge system, so they did **not** put any plan in place for controlling or monitoring information **sent** over the Internet. The system just keeps getting bigger and bigger, with more and more people using it.

There is an **Internet** Society (ISOC), which sets standards to help the Internet run smoothly, **but** no one actually monitors or edits the information transmitted over the Internet. There are hundreds of millions of **Web** pages on the Internet (with thousands being added each day). It would not be **possible** for editors to read and monitor all that information. Even if it were, think how much it would cost to hire them!

Could computers be used in some way to **monitor** accuracy on the Internet? Not yet. They are not sophisticated enough to know the difference between what is true and what is not, so it is up to users to learn to tell the difference themselves.

Also, monitoring information sent over the Internet would destroy the **freedom** of the system. However, the price for this freedom is that inaccurate **information** can be sent back and forth just as easily as accurate **information**. Therefore, it is up to Internet users to be aware of possible problems.

■ Internet Crossword Puzzle (page 23)

Chapter 2

■ Who's Who on the World Wide Web (page 32)

Pomona College—*www.Pomona.edu*

American Red Cross—*www.redcross.org*

Ford Motor Company—*www.Ford.com*

World Wildlife Fund—*www.panda.org*

United States Senate—*www.senate.gov*

Petsmart—*www.petsmart.com*

Washington State University—*www.wsu.edu*

Federal Reserve Board—*www.federalreserve.gov*

AYSO—*www.soccer.org*

United States Air Force—*www.af.mil*

Schwinn Bicycles—*www.schwinn.com*

Wal-Mart—*www.walmart.com*

American Society for the Prevention of Cruelty to Animals—*www.aspca.org*

■ Keep Your Eyes on the Goal! (page 33)

1. **H** = *www.americanrevolutioncollege.edu*
2. **O** = *www.preserveourmusic.org*
3. **P** = *www.reveremonument.gov*
4. **P** = *www.usmilitarybands.mil*
5. **H** = *www.rememberthesoldiers.org*
6. **O** = *www.revoluntionarytimeline.edu*
7. **H** = *www.historicmaps.com*
8. **Y** = *www.flagsflagsflags.com*
9. **I** = *www.geographyclass.edu*
10. **I** = *www.oldtymestore.com*
11. **R** = *www.historiccookingschool.edu*
12. **A** = *www.nationallibrary.gov*

"Hip, Hip, Hooray, you helped save the day!"

■ Chapter 2 Review (page 34)

1. The Web
2. Web site
3. URL
4. hypertext link
5. home page
6. domain name
7. registrar
8. server
9. browser
10. search engine

Chapter 3

■ Expertise Activity (page 43)

1. DDS or DMD
2. RN (or LVN)
3. DVM
4. MD
5. ThD
6. ME
7. CE
8. MFCC
9. JD
10. MDiv
11. B Arch

■ WinnerInternet (page 44)

1. "The Anatomy of a Horse" by Dr. Barnstable, DVM.
2. "Crime and Its Consequences" by John Doe, LLD.
3. "Native American Religious Traditions Before Columbus" by Abe Smith, MDiv.
4. "How to Get Along with your Father" by Myson Allen, MFCC
5. "How to Build Your Own Log Cabin" by Monty Mann, B Arch.

Chapter 6

■ Is That Really So? (page 64)

1. M
2. S
3. M
4. T
5. E
6. Y
7. S
8. O
9. I
10. E
11. S
12. E
13. N
14. O

Is That Really So?
Sometimes "YES," Sometimes "NO."

Chapter 7

■ Hoaxes Note-taking Sheet (page 77)

Unscrambled quote:
A fool and his money are soon parted.

■ Situation Cards (pages 83–84)

- **Situation #1: HOAX**

  Reasoning: Magazine titles are not given. Situation demands that action be taken immediately. Asks you to publicize the information to everyone you know. There is no way to verify the truth of the message, or even an address to which you can send donations. This scenario is based on a real hoax from the 1880s. For more information, read "The Great Duck Egg Fake" in *Alaska Journal* 1977(2): 88–94.

- **Situation #2: REAL**

  Reasoning: The name of the organization requesting money is the local zoo. They give a clear reason for their request. There is no threat that anything bad will happen to you if you don't participate. There is a phone number and a person's name to contact for more information, or to make a donation.

- **Situation #3: HOAX**

  Reasoning: The name of the farmer is not given, only a general location. Encourages you to hurry up and go see it. Threatens that you will miss it if you don't hurry. Mentioning the sheriff and the University tries to create a sense of authenticity, but neither one is quoted or named. Asks for a monetary donation.

- **Situation #4: REAL**

  Reasoning: Although the plea is urgent, a good reason is clearly stated. There is a name, phone number and address to go to for more information or to help with the request. Although the situation states that something bad might happen if people don't help, the reason is clearly stated.

- **Situation #5: REAL**

  Reasoning: An urgent problem is mentioned, but people are asked to act as individuals, not demanded to inform all of their friends. Money is requested for club dues, but not as a donation to an individual. The name and purpose of the organization are clearly stated. People are invited to attend a meeting in a local location.

- **Situation #6: HOAX**

  Reasoning: Makes an emotional claim without supporting it with facts. Asks people to act right away. Uses a General Delivery address instead of a permanent address. Since no address or phone number is given, it would be hard to verify whether the person, or the society, really existed.

- **Situation #7: HOAX**

  Reasoning: It is unlikely the government would sell the Lincoln Memorial. The date of the newspaper is April 1, April Fool's Day. Note: This situation is based on a real April Fool's Joke. On April 1, 1996, the Taco Bell Restaurant chain took out a full page ad in The New York Times claiming that they were buying the Liberty Bell in Philadelphia, and that they would rename it the Taco Liberty Bell. At noon that day, they held a press conference and admitted that it was an April Fool's joke. The White House soon made its own announcement about the Lincoln Memorial, which was also an April Fool's joke.

- **Situation #8: REAL**

  Reasoning: The name of a student at a school is mentioned; it would be easy to verify whether he is a real person. The message invites you to an event at a local restaurant, another way to verify its validity. The message asks for donations to be sent to a known hospital, not to an unknown individual. The message states that receipts will be given. There is a real reason for this message to be urgent.

Chapter 8

■ Chat Room True or False (page 91)

1.	T	7.	T
2.	T	8.	T
3.	T	9.	T
4.	F	10.	T.
5.	T	11.	T
6.	T		

■ NetiQuiz (page 94)

1. a
2. b
3. c
4. b
5. b
6. b

Bibliography

Block, Marylaine. "Gullible's Travels," *NETconnect*, Spring, 2002.

Brimmer, Larry Dane. *The World Wide Web*. Children's Press, 2000.

Burke, John. *A Beginner's Guide to Searching the Internet*. Neal-Schuman Publisher, 1999.

Downing, Douglas, Ph.D., Michael Covington, Ph.D., and Melody Mauldin Covington. *Dictionary of Computer and Internet Terms, Seventh Edition*. Barron's Educational Series, Inc., 2000.

Elliott, Rebecca S., Ph.D., and James Elliott, M.A. *Painless Research Projects*. Barron's Educational Series, Inc., 1998.

Gralla, Preston. *How the Internet Works, Sixth Edition*. QUE, 2002.

Hallet, Vicky. "Extra! Extra! Life on Moon!" *U.S. News & World Report*, August 26/September 2, 2002.

Heiligman, Deborah. *The New York Public Library Kid's Guide to Research*. Scholastic Reference, 1998.

Henderson, Harry. *The Internet*. Lucent Books, 1998.

Kleiner, Carolyn. "Artful Dodgers," *U.S. News & World Report*, August 26/September 2, 2002.

Marsh, Dr. Merle M. *A Student Guide to Misinformation on the Web: Finding Accurate Information for Reports & Papers*. Children's Software Press, 2000.

Rowland, Fytton. "The Librarian's Role in the Electronic Information Environment." www.bodley.ox.ac.uk/icsu/rowlandppr.htm.

Wolinsky, Art. *The History of the Internet and the World Wide Web*. Enslow Publishers, 1999

Web sites from which selected information was used:

http://acro.Harvard.edu/GEI/smileys.html

www.computingcorner.com/help/emoticons/emailabb.htm

www.hoaxbusters.org

www.nonprofit.net/hoax/hoax_big.html

www.iss.stthomas.edu/evaluate.htm

www.icann.org/general/faq1.htm